DESIGN, NATURE, AND REVOLUTION

Design,
Nature,
and
Revolution

Toward a Critical Ecology

Tomás Maldonado

Translated by Mario Domandi
Foreword by Larry Busbea

University of Minnesota Press
Minneapolis

Published by the University of Minnesota Press
111 Third Avenue South, Suite 290
Minneapolis, MN 55401-2520
http://www.upress.umn.edu

Printed in the United States of America on acid-free paper

The University of Minnesota is an equal-opportunity educator and employer.

25 24 23 22 21 20 19   10 9 8 7 6 5 4 3 2 1

Library of Congress Cataloging-in-Publication Data
Maldonado, Tomás, author. | Domandi, Mario, translator.
Design, nature, and revolution : toward a critical ecology / Tomás Maldonado ; translated from the Italian by Mario Domandi.
Other titles: Speranza progettuale. English
Minneapolis : University of Minnesota Press, 2019. | Includes bibliographical references and index.
Identifiers: LCCN 2018039543 | ISBN 978-1-5179-0700-6 (pb)
Subjects: LCSH: Human ecology. | Environmental policy. | Planning.
Classification: LCC GF41 .M3413 2019 | DDC 304.2—dc23
LC record available at https://lccn.loc.gov/2018039543

CONTENTS

Foreword

MALDONADO'S ENVIRONMENT

Larry Busbea

IF WE HOPE TO GRASP the contemporary significance of Tomás Maldonado's intense—and abstruse—half-century-old text, we must recuperate an understanding of *environment (ambiente)* that has been historically eclipsed. When Maldonado used the term, he did not mean (as his translator implied) nature. He intended instead both a more general and more specific state of affairs in which technology, culture, and global ecosystems might be visualized and modeled as mutually generative processes, and perhaps even *forms*. This more integral notion of environment seems relevant once again as designers, cultural theorists, and historians grapple with the political and ecological ramifications of ever more complex and hybrid networks—systems that don't just exist "out there" in the world but constantly and actively mediate our interactions with it.

Perhaps it isn't surprising that Maldonado would be one of the first to articulate such a conception of environment. His professional trajectory had placed him at the very fulcrum of modernity; he was a recipient of its avant-garde aesthetic aspirations and one of the key progenitors of its postindustrial transformation. Accordingly, Maldonado's environment marked the point of overlap at which the reality of the world met the human capacity to transform it. His focus on this point of contact rendered the various terms he analyzed mere abstractions: nature, revolution, and design equally. These words did not denote stable entities but rather became the indices of the technical power and ethical failure of modern human activity. Nature was hopelessly nostalgic. Revolution was ultimately cynical. Design, however, though it had been abused and overly systematized, still held out some ambivalent degree of hope. (Here we might recall the original Italian title of this essay, *La speranza progettuale*—a labor of hope, perhaps, pace Ernst Bloch.[1])

If these observations seem conditional, it is because *Design, Nature, and Revolution* was less a coherent theoretical statement than the diary of an unresolved intellectual struggle.[2] The struggle was not the author's alone. It gripped an entire generation of designers and other cultural producers in the wake of the political eruptions of 1968. This struggle entailed an easy sympathy with the rejection of dominant power structures and a less easy grappling with the types of complicity that rejection revealed. Maldonado felt both of these sentiments acutely. He was in a state of transition after disentangling himself from the directorship of the failing Hochschule für Gestaltung Ulm, or the Ulm School, passing through a lectureship at the Royal College of Arts in London, serving as chairman of the executive committee of ICSID (an international conglomeration of design associations), and occupying a visiting appointment at the School of Architecture at Princeton University (this book was derived from his lectures there)—all between 1965 and 1970.

The book broke apart. Originally conceived as a kind of systematic treatise on design science or method, the text disintegrated into a terse glossary of critical terminology of the moment: technocracy, planning, alienation, ecology, systems, critique, semiology, dialectic, theory, praxis (not to mention design, nature, and revolution). It became an existential and intellectual account of the author's attempt to reconcile the Anglophone tradition

viii

of pragmatism (from Defoe to Peirce), which had inspired him in so many ways, with Continental modes of *ideologiekritic* and poststructuralism. As he mapped and recorded his reading in these areas, the endnotes took on a life of their own; often they manifested a more eloquent and lyrical life than the main body of the text.

The book's "lack of homogeneity" (xvii), in the end, would consign it to an uncertain place in the history of both design and environment. It was translated into several languages yet wasn't widely read or cited in any of them.[3] In the United States, it was drowned out, perhaps, by the 1972 publication of several more resounding design and ecological texts: Robert Venturi, Denise Scott Brown, and Steven Izenour's *Learning from Las Vegas*; Victor Papanek's *Design for the Real World*; Gregory Bateson's *Steps to an Ecology of Mind*; and Theodor Roszak's *Where the Wasteland Ends*. That same year Emilio Ambasz, Maldonado's younger compatriot and acolyte, mounted the landmark exhibition *Italy: The New Domestic Landscape* at the Museum of Modern Art in New York. Maldonado's anguished deliberations on the ethics of systems theory, social alienation, and the "fashion of ecology" could hardly stand up to these polemical statements and seductive displays.[4]

Most contemporary accounts remember *Design, Nature, and Revolution* for its incisive Marxist and semiotic critiques of two extremes of design culture around 1970: the techno-utopian vision of Buckminster Fuller and the blithe acceptance of the architecture of capitalism on the part of Venturi and Scott Brown. Although these two paradigms are seldom discussed in tandem, Maldonado saw them as analogous in their lack of political consciousness. Fuller disingenuously replaced political considerations with technical ones. The results were nightmarish domes: insular, artificial, "suboptimized" environments. *Learning from Las Vegas*, on the other hand, eschewed politics by cynically taking the communicative function of the signage on the Strip at face value and failing to see the ways in which capital itself had ordered the arrangement of the city on the ground. In both instances, according to Maldonado, ecological complexity had been reduced to a single element (whether climatization or communication). A near future and altogether too close present had been substituted for a concern with deeper developmental trends and historical realities. Neither project employed a nuanced "sociological imagination" or a "critical ecology" to map, assess, and plan the human environment.

With its condemnation of the "scandal of society," or environmental pollution and degradation, Maldonado's book has also served as a kind of suppressed political conscience for the ecological aspects of design.[5] It is frequently mentioned in surveys of the history of design and environment, even though its precise impact is difficult to establish. This is likely because Maldonado's conception of environment was so capacious: equal parts nature, technology, and politics. Our understanding of environment—until quite recently—has seldom been as inclusive. In this sense, Maldonado's discourse more closely resembles that of Bruno Latour than Rachel Carson.

As Maldonado said in one of his lectures at Princeton in 1966, "It is a fact that there exist not only 'inanimate environment agents' but also 'animate environment agents,'" and that both would by necessity equally figure in any new conception of "environmental design."[6] Indeed, this last concept would drive his thinking during this period, both inspiring (and disrupting) the present text. For Maldonado, environmental design held a distinct potential for both the pedagogy and practice of design writ large. As it did for many of his colleagues on both sides of the Atlantic, it held out hope for a design method freed from subjective sensibilities and an obsessive attention to the formal properties of objects (which, truth be told, persisted at the Bauhaus, and at Ulm). It promised that design might detach itself from its position of servitude vis-à-vis both art and industry, not in order to become autonomous but rather to become a privileged intermedial translator among all fields of human activity—among all systems, animate and inanimate, scientific and humanistic, natural and cultural.

But for Maldonado (and here he broke from many of those advocating "design methods," or what would circa 1968 become institutionalized "Environmental Design"), such shifts did *not* entail the total rejection of aesthetics.[7] It was still the task of design to "give sense and structure to the human environment."[8] It was still necessary to account for the ways in which the world becomes sensible to the subject, "the delicate operation of transforming a philosophical notion into a fact of sensibility, a scientific construct into a fact of perception" (5). In this sense, (environmental) design was less about an objective optimization of natural and cultural systems than it was an attempt to acknowledge "the most subtle and hidden aspects of our mediating membrane" (5). After all, this was precisely what Maldonado had been attempting to reconcile since his earliest encounters with the avant-garde—the tensions between perception and reality, between objectivity and subjectivity, and between determinism and agency. This was what he had admired in his benefactor Max Bill as the latter's "will of coherence": his "desire to promote a new and integral method for the interpretation and creation of the visual events of our time."[9]

But the "will of coherence" that Bill would channel into a concrete "good form" Maldonado would turn toward the identification of patterns and relations among environmental scales and systems. He would be drawn to methods (cybernetics, semiotics, systems theory, programming, planning, management) that promised to trace the threads holding these systems together in a certain order, or grammar. And while it would be impossible to describe these patterns as stable forms, it was nonetheless the myriad but structured ways in which they interacted and became sensible to the subject that was the proper object of design for Maldonado. Another way of saying this might be: to design *in* an environment is to design *an* environment. *Design, Nature, and Revolution* is an intense reckoning with both the impossibility and inevitability of this state of affairs.

NOTES

1. Ernst Bloch, *The Principle of Hope*, 3 vols., trans. Neville Plaice, Stephen Plaice, and Paul Knight (Cambridge, Mass.: MIT Press, 1986 [1954]).

2. The book also marks the moment that Maldonado transitioned from corporate design projects to cultural criticism and the editorial and teaching activities that would occupy him as an Italian citizen (since 1967). For an account of his work and publications in Italy, see Raimonda Riccini, "The Italian Experience," in *Tomás Maldonado* (Milan: Skira, 2009), 156–77, and Raimonda Riccini, "Tomás Maldonado and the Impact of the Hochschule für Gestaltung Ulm in Italy," in Grace Lees-Maffei and Kjetil Fallan, eds., *Made in Italy: Rethinking a Century of Italian Design* (London: Bloomsbury Press, 2014), 89–105.

3. The most sensitive reading of the English edition may have been Lawrence Alloway, "*Design, Nature, and Revolution: Toward a Critical Ecology,*" *Artforum* (September 1973): 74–75. A more recent analysis is Simon Sadler, "A Container and Its Contents: Re-reading Tomás Maldonado's *Design, Nature, and Revolution: Toward a Critical Ecology,*" *Room One Thousand* 1 (2013): 41–53.

4. This was also the year that Ambasz attempted to realize Maldonado's call to establish a pedagogical model for "environmental design" with his *Universitas* project at MoMA. See Emilio Ambasz, ed., *The Universitas Project: Solutions for a Post-Technological Society* (New York: The Museum of Modern Art, 2006). On the relationship between Maldonado's work and Ambasz's various initiatives at MoMA, see Felicity D. Scott, *Architecture or Techno-Utopia: Politics after Modernism* (Cambridge, Mass.: MIT Press, 2007), 89–115. Victor Margolin has observed that *Design, Nature, and Revolution* was "barely noticed" in the United States as it was "overshadowed by the [MoMA] show's emphasis on elegant objects and avant-garde projects." Victor Margolin, "Postwar Design Literature: A Preliminary Map-

ping," in Victor Margolin, ed., *Design Discourse: History, Theory, Criticism* (Chicago: University of Chicago Press, 1989), 279, note 14.

5. Paul Betts has read it as a kind of apology on the part of the design establishment for its role in environmental degradation. Paul Betts, *The Authority of Everyday Objects* (Berkeley: University of California Press, 2004), 256.

6. Tomás Maldonado, "How to Fight Complacency in Design Education," *Ulm* 17–18 (1966): 15.

7. In this sense, architect Alan Colquhoun's critique of Maldonado's Princeton seminar was somewhat off the mark. He argued that "beneath the apparent objectivity of [Maldonado's] ideas there lies an aesthetic doctrine" (71). Alan Colquhoun, "Typology and Design Method," *Perspecta* 12 (1969): 71–74. Maldonado would not have disagreed, frankly. While he opposed the overreliance on conventional forms (preestablished building types or type objects) within design, he fully understood design's role in aesthetically mediating the human experience of reality. For Maldonado, the aesthetic did not inhere in an object but shaped the structure of an environmental relation; it existed in the ensemble of objects, at the level of metadesign. For more on this concept, see Larry Busbea, "Metadesign: Object and Environment in France, c. 1970," *Design Issues* 25, no. 4 (Autumn 2009): 103–19.

8. Maldonado, "How to Fight Complacency," 18.

9. Tomás Maldonado, *Max Bill* (Buenos Aires: Nueva Visión, 1955), 13.

PREFACE TO THE AMERICAN EDITION

I HAVE DECIDED to leave the text of this essay unchanged, except for a few insignificant modifications. But I did think it necessary to add a postscript and a few additional notes, for particular reasons.

In January, 1970, when the Italian edition of this book was being printed, the problem of the degradation of the environment, which is the principal theme of the book, suddenly became the center of general interest. In the postscript, written a year later, I shall try to assess the true significance of this phenomenon.

With the new notes, I hope to fill some of the important lacunae of the first edition. I am referring in particular to certain arguments on which I failed to give a conclusive judgment. I did not want to take a position on issues that was not susceptible to objective analysis.

I forgot that such precautions, though legitimate, often lead to results that are the exact opposite of those intended, i.e., to uncertain, inexplicit, almost reluctant thoughts. The field is left open to arbitrary interpretations, which produce mortifying misunderstandings. For example: compliments from our congenial adversaries and censure from our congenial allies.

xv

In this noisy age, it is hard to listen. Ernst Bloch lamented recently: "Who listens? . . . Applause from the wrong side. Criticism for the wrong side . . ." To avoid being misheard, or heard incorrectly, we must take fewer of the precautions mentioned earlier. The new notes pursue this aim. In particular, those on violence (page 93), on the relationship between city and country (page 109), and on the possibility of a general theory of design praxis (page 127).

They are long notes, and they therefore make even more obvious the embarrassing lack of proportion between text and notes already evident in the original edition. Even more than before, the book threatens to split in two: on the one hand the essay, the principal text; on the other hand the "scrapbook"—that is, the author's comments, reflections, and bibliographical notes before, during, and after the main essay. I hope the reader will accept this rather unorthodox composition without anxiety (or worse, annoyance). For his convenience, he may read the essay first, and then the notes. It is important that the essay be read sequentially; not so for the notes.

Milan
January, 1971

PREFACE

THE GENERAL APPEARANCE of this essay may well be considered unusual. In fact, it will probably be hard to see any reason for its disorderly and fragmentary structure, its variety of approaches, and its constant movement from objective to subjective discourse, from detached academic argumentation to the violent harshness of polemical commitment.

The lack of homogeneity can, I hope, be explained by the tortuous road I had to take before arriving at this destination. When I started, my ambitious idea had been to write a complete, systematic book on the present state of methodological research in the field of environmental design and planning. But when I had completed a good part of the work and was in full swing, I ceased to believe in the undertaking. In fact, the more I learned about present methodological techniques, the more clearly did I perceive a contradiction: These sophisticated techniques are relatively mature, whereas the decision-making centers of power in our society, those who are supposed to make reasonable use of the techniques, are absolutely immature. I had wanted to write a treatise, but I suddenly understood that it was an illusion. You cannot write a treatise on a reality that is not factually treatable.

And so, at that point, I felt justified in changing my plans. Instead of a systematic book, I thought it wiser to publish a brief polemical essay on the flagrant contradiction I had encountered. Nevertheless, the original plan left its traces on this text, causing the lack of homogeneity alluded to earlier.

I should like to emphasize that a large part of the essay has been written as a response—for better or for worse—to the ideas stirred up recently by the revolutionary movement of revolt among the young. So far as my position on this matter is concerned, I do not think I have allowed myself to be influenced either by those who are always ready to exalt the revolt of the young or by those who always condemn it. Without any doubt, we must be grateful to youth for having awakened us from our somnolence.

They have reminded us that ours is not an Arcadian epoch, but rather a painfully convulsed age. Nevertheless, the mistake many young people make is continually and obstinately to refuse to hope. They do not want to admit that the true exercise of critical consciousness is inseparable from the will to search for a coherent, articulated, and planned alternative to the convulsions of our era. Not that I have been so pretentious here as to postulate such an alternative in all its details. My effort has been more modest. I have only tried to accomplish a preliminary goal, a "reconnaissance," as they say in the military, of the area in which such an alternative may be found in the future. But "reconnaissance" presupposes clarification, the removal of anything that might confound the accuracy of our observation and therefore of our assessment. That explains why a part of this essay has been dedicated to the definition of terms; another to a critical examination of the causes behind the various currents of nihilism so fashionable today; and finally, still another to a denunciation of the more typical current forms of mystification that surround planning.

The fact that no prescriptions are offered should not surprise the reader. The enormity of the problems that face us today in the field of environmental design and planning counsels us to use extreme caution in passing from descriptive to prescriptive discourse. Many times in the past decade architects and urban planners have failed to exercise such caution; and the consequences have been rather grave. This essay is merely an attempt to point out the errors to be avoided.

I want to thank my students at the Hochschule für Gestaltung, Ulm, and my students at the School of Architecture, Princeton University, with whom I discussed many of the arguments presented here at great length.

I am particularly grateful to Marisa Bertoldini, who helped me in the preparation of the Italian manuscript.

Milan
January, 1970

Chapter One

ENVIRONMENT, NATURE, ALIENATION

FROM TIME IMMEMORIAL—or at least since the time man could be called man—we have lived in an environment partly constructed by ourselves.

Paradoxically, though, we have only recently become aware of the existence of such an environment; we have only recently become conscious of the rather obvious fact that we are surrounded and conditioned by a world specifically ours, by a physical and sociocultural surrounding now termed the "human environment."[1]*

The whole speculative impulse and systematic zeal of traditional philosophy from Aristotle to Hegel was directed at first toward an exhaustive treatment of the relationship between man and nature. Later, it moved toward the relationship between man and man, and still later to the relationship between man and history. But philosophy ignored the "human environment," the reality that for centuries represented the concrete world in which we made our anguished efforts to live, cohabit, and survive.[2]

With no more than a superficial glance at the evolution of thought from Hegel onward, we can identify the most

* Notes begin on page 79.

1

important of the early reactions to the attitude we have just described. We can see it best in the basic ideas of the great thinkers who had the most influence on Western culture during that period. It is there, for example, in the Hegelian-Feuerbachian-Marxian concept of alienation, a concept that has helped us to see the dialectical connection between consciousness and social reality in a new light. It is present in the provocative insights of C. S. Peirce, which opened the way for current research on the sign function of environmental structures. It is there in the formidable, demystifying assault carried out by Nietzsche, who was obsessively hostile to any dogma that glorified the passivity and acquiescence of man in the universe. It is in the distilled phenomenological methodology of the later Husserl, from which we can still expect fundamental clarifications of the structure of our immediate reality. It is present in the courageous action of Freud, who with one blow severed all those sacred links between individual psychic life and cultural environment. It is in the efforts of the representatives of modern empiricism, who polemically refute any and all forms of metaphysics in philosophizing about the objective world. Finally, it is present in the philosophers of existence, who take the position that human life defines (and redefines) itself as a function of the contingencies and environmental situations in which it evolves, and never with the aid of categories that claim to be absolute.

These thinkers represent the first efforts to get away from the intimidating, age-old influence of the Adam myth and trauma, which consists in the arbitrary assumption that we passively inherit the human world. But the very opposite is true: The human world is our own realization. What is even more important (to follow the very beaten path of Hegelian-Feuerbachian-Marxian language), our realization of the human world is inseparable from our self-realization as human beings. As a matter of fact, phylogenetically and ontogeneti-

2

cally, the making of our environment and the making of ourselves has been a single process. But if that work is a factor in self-realization, it is also a factor in alienation. It is obvious by now that the particular mode in which consciousness takes hold of environmental reality has a decisive influence on the ultimate configuration of that reality. To put it another way: If there be a consciousness that is disjointed, enfeebled, and even humiliated by alienation, there will always be a corresponding environmental reality that is decipherable only in terms of alienation. But all of this is true only on a very general level. Those who have tried to treat the problem with rigorous analysis have all arrived at the same disappointing conclusion—namely, that the idea of alienation has a limited scope and is useful only up to a certain point. Beyond that point, it proves to be vague, inscrutable, and, what is even worse, misleading. Still, we must not make the mistake of denying its value completely. On the contrary, the current resumption of the debate concerning the idea of alienation could open new and fruitful prospects in studying the link between conscious life and environmental life.[3]

Nothing could be more erroneous than to attribute our emerging awareness of the existence and problems of the "human environment" exclusively to the development of philosophical ideas. There are other factors of equal importance. The current conviction, for example, that there is a mediating membrane—the "human environment"—between man and reality, man and himself, and man and history has also been the result of clarification and investigation by the natural scientists.

In the last century these men established the basic principles of general ecology,[4] while others in this century have collaborated with sociologists, psychologists, and anthropologists in the development of human (or social)[5] ecology as a new branch of general ecology.

3

Without doubt, a scientific formulation of the problem furnished the best support for those thinkers after Hegel who found it necessary to call the attention of philosophy to the "human environment" and its particular structure. For the ecologists, the "human environment," defined with almost polemical objectivity, is one of the many subsystems that compose the vast ecological system of nature. Still, these ecologists do not hesitate to attribute to our system a very particular kind of "behavior," unique on our planet. The exceptional character of the "human environment" is no anthropocentric fiction. It is evident that our subsystem is distinguished above all by its ability to use (or rather abuse) its relationships with the other subsystems, and to radically influence their destiny. The other subsystems can also disturb a foreign ecological equilibrium; but only ours possesses today the virtual and real capacity of provoking *substantial*—that is, irreversible—disturbances in the equilibrium of other subsystems.

The risk does not end there. Disturbances of this sort are never compartmentalized, for sooner or later they alter the stability of the entire system, not excluding, of course, the subsystem that initiated the disturbance. The factor that plays the role of *agent provocateur*, so to speak, in the ecological universe is none other than man, or, more precisely, man's consciousness operating on his physical and sociocultural surroundings.[6]

At this point we see to what extent the scientific approach to the problem of the "human environment" brings us to the central preoccupation of philosophy after Hegel. Briefly, it is concerned with rendering more intelligible the role of a consciousness confronted with a stubbornly contingent and situational reality. And it is a reality we no longer wish to think about categorically, but rather as a function of the problem within all our problems: the conflict between freedom and necessity.

4

The concept of the "human environment" originates on the one hand in modern philosophy, and on the other in the revolutionary contributions of ecological science. But we must not forget a third source, the literary and artistic description of the "human environment," which carried out the delicate operation of transforming a philosophical notion into a fact of sensibility, a scientific construct into a fact of perception. Indirectly, these narrative efforts have revealed the most subtle and hidden aspects of our mediating membrane. The richness of what we might call the "intuitive" observations in Henry James, Dostoevsky, Proust, Kafka, Italo Svevo, and Joyce furnish the material that must be used in the future in careful studies based on this viewpoint.[7]

The same can be said of the formidable amount of visual environmental material accumulated in our century first by photography, and then by movies and television.[8]

Nor can we fail to point out the role played in the progress of our environmental awareness by those tangible structures that have so profoundly conditioned our individual and social behavior "psychosomatically," so to speak. I am alluding to physical structures such as cities, buildings, and objects of use which have helped give cultural form and content to our surroundings.

Chapter Two

HUMAN ECOLOGY AND
DIALECTIC OF THE CONCRETE

UP TO THIS POINT, our task has been to hazard an initial hypothesis, approximate, fragmentary, and speculative though it may be, concerning the fundamental motives that have brought us to our present consciousness of the "human environment."

Having done that, we obviously do not claim to have solved, but on the contrary only posed, the problem we should like to discuss. In other words, we believe we have arrived close to the fundamental question: What, in the final analysis, is "the human environment"? Is it the result of a blind process, absolutely devoid of intent and coherence, an arbitrary and desultory accumulation of isolated facts, an uncontrolled and uncontrollable phenomenon?

The spectacle offered us by our present environment seems, at first, to support that interpretation. In fact, anyone living in this world with his eyes open cannot fail to recognize that our hypothetical reality is very similar to the reality we see and endure every day. It is a reality in which the relationships of men to objects has reached an exasperating degree of irrationality.[1]

Still, a more careful analysis reveals clearly that this des-

6

cription, though correct in appearance, rests on very question-
able premises. We can (and must) denounce the irrationality
of our environment; but no discussion of its alienating nature
can make us forget what we have already seen—namely, that
it is the result of our factual will, and that all of us make the
objects that surround us, which in turn constitute a determining part of our human condition.[2]

Our relationship with the environment in which we live is
comparable, say, to the relationship between a container and
its contents, each of which has developed independently of
the other. Such a relationship may or may not imply a re-
ciprocal correspondence. Ours is always a relationship of correspondence—which does not rule out the possibility that such
a relationship (as often happens) can turn out to be substantially negative for us and our environment. And yet there is
no doubt that here the container and the contents, the human
condition and the human environment, are the result of one
and the same dialectical process, one and the same process of
mutual conditioning and formation.

It is because of this process that we can become an active
and creative part of factual reality. In the final analysis, it is
precisely in this connection with the environment that we
have always stubbornly sought (though not always found) the
satisfaction of one of our most profound needs as living beings
—that is to say, our need for *concrete projection*, for confirma-
tion of the final tangibility of all that we are, do, and want to
do in the world.

Having reached this point, it is necessary to call into question a philosophy, or rather an attitude, very fashionable today, that sees fit to deny completely the value of concrete
projection. Supporters of that position use these arguments:
The human need for concrete projection, they say, is a result
of the relatively recent utopian, rationalistic, and enlightened
tradition, though its deeper root must be sought in the mani-

7

acal forms of aggressive activism and utilitarianism of Western culture in general, and of bourgeois society in particular.

The counterpart of this aberrant and alienating need would be *transcendental projection*, the extreme form of subjectivism which (still according to those supporters) has been, in every epoch, the expression of the contemplative wisdom and the refined knowledge which permeates Oriental culture.

The attempt to drastically polarize the human need for projection (concrete and Western on the one hand, transcendental and Oriental on the other) does not strike us as an example of logical incisiveness or of historical precision. In fact, it represents a deplorable feebleness of thought, a concoction that throws the most banal preconceptions of the historiography of the last century together with the greatest equivocations of Spenglerian cosmography. That in turn gives rise to problems that are irremediably anachronistic, and at the same time difficult if not impossible to solve.

For here we have not only the grossly oversimplified problem of the "conceptions of the world" dichotomy, but also the even more grossly oversimplified problem of the "Western-Oriental" dichotomy. History belies any such pretense at an absolutely symmetrical correlation between two opposed conceptions of the world, between two opposed geocultural configurations.

In historical development of the cultures called Western and Oriental we find examples of the most radical objectivism and the most radical subjectivism; in each we find as much highly inventive technical-mechanical genius as we find bold, abstract-speculative genius; there is as much sensual adherence to the world as there is ascetic condemnation of the world.[3]

The alternative "concrete projection or abstract projection" is a false alternative. But neither are we yet convinced of the validity of the Marxist thesis, inherited directly from German Idealism and Romanticism, according to which concreteness

8

and transcendence can become two different modalities of one and the same theme. Less ambiguously, it holds that transcendental projection (inasmuch as it is a univocal, isolated, and individual undertaking of the human spirit) can, indeed must, disappear in the future, to become part of the fabric of concrete projection.

One thing, at any rate, seems clear and incontestable: Man has never been and never will be able to live without concrete projection. Those who want, nowadays, to cast concrete projection aside not only misunderstand man's past, they compromise his future.

Here we come to an argument we consider fundamental. The rejection of concrete projection also implies the rejection of design planning,* for the latter cannot exist without the former. In other words, we cannot build models that allow us to simulate structures, actions, and behavior if we do not already possess an unequivocal will to realize such structures, actions, and behavior.

All of this is rather obvious, and the attempt to deny it with the help of mere verbal artifices has not yet met with success. Without question, the facts are particularly stubborn on this score, and they are hard to ignore. Nevertheless, all of this can be more or less mystified with impunity, except for one thing —no one can deny that design and planning are the most solid nexus joining man to reality and history.

Obviously, our environmental reality, whether it be examined globally, in sectors, or at specific points, is the result of what Vico called "the ability to make"; it is the link between the *verum* and the *factum*.[4] If it is not legitimate to identify the "ability to make" with what might be called "the ability

---

* Translator's Note: The author has used the word *progettazione*, which has been translated as two words, design and planning, depending on the meaning. The word "design" is used in a conceptual sense; the word "planning" is used in an operative sense. Both words are used together when the emphasis and meaning are both conceptual and operational.

to design," we must at least admit that both expressions belong to the same order of discourse—that is, to the world of man's operative discourse.

Surely, making and designing do not mutually presuppose each other, but then they are very rarely found independent of one another, and only very rarely do they not participate in the same volitional and factual modality of acting within reality.

A typical example of doing without designing is to be found in play (of doing that usually prescinds from any rational plan formulated *a priori*). And a typical example of designing without doing is to be found in the idea of utopia (of design in which the basic goal is not immediate realization).

In this (and only in this) context, we are speaking of play as free, spontaneous activity; we are speaking of play without a pre-established code, without the "rules of the game," without a system of reinforcements or punishments that might suffocate the freedom of the player. Utopia, as we shall see later, can be defined in very different ways. For the moment, and very provisionally, we are speaking of it, too, as a free and spontaneous activity, not subjected to the exigencies of the "here and now," and without any imposition of immediate verisimilitude or plausibility. Obviously, there is a link between play and utopia: gratuitousness. Still, it is not an absolute gratuitousness, for both can be considered, to a certain extent, preparatory exercises: play for doing, and utopia for designing.

On the other hand, as Ernst Bloch[5] points out, utopia has a component that is missing in play: In most cases, the moving force behind utopia is hope. Without doubt, positive utopian thought (we are not concerned with the negative conceptions, ranging from Samuel Butler[6] to Arno Schmidt[7]) implies a recognition that the world, though imperfect, is perfectible. It

10

is, therefore, a very subtle form of concrete projection; not a real, but certainly a virtual form.

No wonder then that dialogue is still possible with the utopians—at least with some of them. And that of itself is not negligible, for in our day, dialogue between cultured men is becoming ever more infrequent and difficult, and the tyranny of a new Manichean obscurantism leads us ever more to attribute all ideas and words to some concealed client.

The utopians, of course, have chosen to flee forward. They have taken on the ambiguous task (at once a trap and a springboard) of making up a history of the future, of designing the map of a world as yet undiscovered, or, perhaps, yet to be invented. Still, it cannot be denied that such stirring of innovative (even if chimerical) courage has always, or almost always, contained a formidable revolutionary charge. Dialogue with the utopians is feasible because, as we already pointed out, in spite of any and all shadings, their basic moving force is always hope. Nevertheless, our hopes need not necessarily be the same. On the contrary, it is sometimes preferable that they not be.

If dialogue *is* possible, it certainly cannot take place with those who for some time now have looked upon the "principle of hope" as merely the fossilized residue of a sentimental ideology. They are the ones who reject not only dialogue, but also the value and practice of designing and planning in all their modalities. When we have hope in something, we also have something to say to ourselves; so, too, designing and planning become superfluous when we have nothing to hope for, nothing to say to ourselves.

Whereas hope without planning (and we repeat, we are referring to transcendental projection) is a very particular form of alienated behavior, planning without hope is its most typical form. In other words, it is the paradoxical behavior that results from being forced to plan without having anything

11

concrete to plan, And what is more, to do so without hope, without will.[8]

In our opinion, Sisyphus furnishes an exact allegorical representation of the designer without hope. The "alienated" behavior of the designer in bourgeois society, living "in the greatest discomfort and in the most paralyzing frustration," has been lucidly analyzed by C. Wright Mills in his essay *Man in the Middle: The Designer.*[9]

Chapter Three

RATIONALITY AND REPRESSION

HAVING TRIED TO SHOW that the worldwide rejection of planning as action without hope is amply justified, we shall now try to specify the causes that have brought about this crisis of hope in planning. According to one of the most common interpretations, the crisis is a result of the ever-growing critical and negative attitude toward consumer civilization. Undoubtedly, such an attitude implies a direct accusation against planning; or, more precisely, against the planners, who are singled out as the bearers of responsibility for conceiving, programming, deciding, and producing our actual environmental reality.

Very frequently the polemic against consumer civilization shows a tendency to sacrifice hope in planning too completely and too readily. Still, we cannot say that such an interpretation is essentially wrong; rather, it becomes wrong because of its unilateral approach.[1]

Obviously, "nihilism in planning" cannot be understood in isolation. It needs to be examined in the context of two other phenomena which, as we all know, are taking on a particularly virulent form everywhere: cultural nihilism and political nihilism.

We must acknowledge that T. W. Adorno, with one of his dazzling aphorisms, has opened up one possibility for integral reflection on the subject before us. In his last book, *Negative Dialektik*,[2] Adorno picks up once again an argument he had already discussed in his earlier essays. "All culture after Auschwitz . . . is garbage." With that, he is not just trying to re-emphasize the atrocious nature of the Nazi (or, if you will, German) crime; beyond that, he is arguing that even if everyone in the future were to forget the enormity of the crime, one scar at least would not heal: the scar left by Auschwitz on the body of modern enlightened culture—that is to say, the conviction that rationality can be used as an instrument in the service of the most brutal irrationality.

In other words, after Auschwitz, after the moral scandal of the rational perfection of genocide, it is no longer possible to "make culture" as we did before. We can no longer continue to "promise," above all because we have lost all credibility before others and before ourselves. What Adorno calls "the philosophy of promising" (*Philosophie des Versprechens*) did not survive the holocaust of the Nazi concentration-camp world. Up to Auschwitz, our prevalently enlightened culture had been guided by several fundamental choices: After Francis Bacon we preferred facts to opinions; after Raimundus Lullus, Thomas Hobbes, and G. W. Leibniz, we preferred calculation to debate.

These choices marked a radical change of perspective in the history of philosophy. They signaled the attempt to bring thought closer to reality by replacing a philosophy that speculated on ideas and often hazarded prescriptive conclusions with a philosophy that operated on facts, and, with the help of calculation, arrived at descriptive conclusions. In the final analysis, it was an attempt to secure the absolute axiological neutrality of thought. Beyond doubt, this attempt opened the way for modern scientific thought. But we must neverthe-

less admit that although highly fruitful, it became an obsession, and ended by becoming an instrument of "bourgeois
coldness" (*bürgerliche Kälte*).

By "bourgeois coldness," Adorno[3] means behavior charac-
terized by absolute negativity, resulting from the attempt to
get axiological neutrality and absolute positives at any cost.
It is the behavior of the detached spectator who looks at the
world with the cold "dry eye" of which Descartes spoke.[4]
Bourgeois coldness reifies, "thingifies" men; in the end, it no
longer perceives their misfortunes, their suffering, or even
their torture. True, the "dry eye" sees far-off things particularly
well; but it fails to distinguish things that are close. What is
worse, it fails to perceive the "wet eyes" of others, even when
they too are close.

That is why the extermination camp at Auschwitz must be
considered the most brutal testimonial of "bourgeois coldness." The implacable pedantry of the files found in the
archives at Auschwitz—facts and calculations in the service
of cruelty—has its clear genealogy in the history of ideas.

Fascism cannot be explained merely as irrationalism (as
nearly all of us once believed). Fascism must be explained as
an excrescence, a neoplasm, though certainly spurious, of the
Enlightenment.[5]

Fundamentally, that is the central thesis of the *Dialektik
der Aufklärung* by Adorno and Horkheimer.[6] The Enlightenment has always harbored within it the seeds of "bourgeois
coldness." We must not fail to assess the importance of that
fact in all its implications, since our present civilization—
technical and scientific—continues to be, as we have already
noted, a civilization inspired for the most part by the Enlightenment. Hardly surprising, then, that in our civilization,
the making of culture, philosophy, science, art, or literature
has become an ambiguous enterprise, since no one can be certain in advance that he is not acting as the accomplice of some

15

potential or actual tyrant. That is to say, no one can be sure that the culture he is helping to form is not, as the Frankfurt philosopher called it, garbage. And the same may be said for politics.

That is the novelty of Auschwitz. Condorcet, the Girondist and man of the Enlightenment, could continue unperturbed to write his *Esquisse d'un tableau historique des progrès de l'esprit humain* while waiting to be guillotined; and that at a time when Robespierre, a Jacobin and a man of the Enlightenment too, had already inaugurated his bloody Reign of Terror. Condorcet probably did not see any relationship between his ideas and the Terror, which, directly or indirectly, had been provoked by those ideas.

Nor does he seem to have been very troubled by the fact that he himself was about to be swept away by the Terror. On the contrary, he continued to write and to discourse on the "progress of the human spirit."

After Auschwitz, an attitude of that sort would be unthinkable. Today, nothing can make us forget that many of the ideas we still believe could lead once again to the same reifying hypnosis that made the Nazi world possible.

Today, we try to prevent that eventuality by renouncing action in favor of action without precise purpose. The results are cultural nihilism and political nihilism, which, when they meet, give birth to nihilism in planning.

At this point, we must ask ourselves a question: Why did this wave of general nihilism burst forth now? Why is it, all of a sudden, that no creative act is worth performing, no idea worth pursuing in depth? Why has this "post-Auschwitz" attitude, latent for a quarter century, re-emerged just now, to become the lacerating reality it is?

Adorno's interpretation does not adequately explain all the implications of the phenomenon. In the final analysis, it is not right to say that Auschwitz is the only cause of the "post-Auschwitz" attitude.

16

Permit us a statement that may seem tautological. The present "post-Auschwitz" attitude is also to be explained by what really and truly comes after Auschwitz. In other words, the reasons must surely be sought in the trauma produced by the enormity of the Nazi concentration-camp massacre; but they must also be sought in all those events that have taken place in these last twenty-five years, and which have deepened the trauma.

With the perspective provided by these two decades, it is both moving and disappointing to look back to the good faith (or ingenuity) of the men who, in 1948, two years after Churchill's speech in Fulton,[7] could still welcome with enthusiasm a *Déclaration universelle des droits de l'homme*,[8] an illusive document that led us to believe in the imminent advent of a world in which the rights of man would be guaranteed and respected. Subsequent events shattered that hope. Without exception, all the rights proclaimed in that document have been cynically denied and annulled in one way or another by the repeated acts of aggression of the great powers.

The historical itinerary of these interventions reveals in an exemplary way the progressive erosion of a model of relations among nations that was supposed to exclude conclusively the sort of politics of which Auschwitz was the most perfect expression and the most logical consequence.

Undoubtedly, the most clamorous and the most jarring of these interventions is the one in Vietnam. Let us understand each other. We do not mean to say that Vietnam alone is responsible for the nihilism rampant in politics, culture, and planning today. For in fact, every intervention against the free self-determination of peoples is equally responsible, whether carried out with the heavy hand of tanks and Napalm, or with the light hand of *coup d'état*.

Nevertheless, the hypocrisy with which the military intervention in Vietnam has masked its aims, and the impudence with which it has realized them, have obviously been the

17

major factors in bringing to a boiling point the worldwide nihilism that other interventions have been preparing for years.

In other words, Vietnam is for the so-called "cold war" what Auschwitz was for the "hot war": the symbol destined to traumatize the moral conscience of men for a long time to come. Vietnam makes Auschwitz real again. A new symbol gives life to an old symbol, a new trauma deepens an old trauma. New bills come to remind us of old bills not yet paid.

Those who refuse to identify the symbol of Vietnam with the symbol of Auschwitz are only partly right. In point of fact, the distance that separates Vietnam from Auschwitz is merely the distance that separates two different phases of one and the same process. Historically, Vietnam comes after Auschwitz; but morally it precedes it. Vietnam contains in embryo all the component parts of Auschwitz; from Vietnam we get to Auschwitz.

Consider the following example: Bob Hope described the Napalm bombings of Vietnamese villages as the best "slum-clearing project" that has ever been carried out.[9]

I do not think we need take very seriously the squalid "black humor" of a Hollywood clown. But we must take very seriously the fact that there is a public ready to laugh at that kind of humor. For it is clear that Bob Hope, a professional when it comes to being funny, would not risk presenting a remark as comical if he were not sure that his public would accept it as such. He would not try to be funny about a subject if he were not certain that his public already found it amusing.

When faced with a spectacle of cruelty,[10] there are the following alternatives: condemnation, applause, or indifference. The history of cruelty (or cruelty in history) teaches us that whenever condemnation, either for objective or subjective reasons, is not possible, sooner or later applause will come, almost always by way of a transitory stage of indifference.

18

Nevertheless, the passage from indifference to applause has never been simple: it has always required a particular kind of help—the joke, the rendering ridiculous of the victim, the object of cruelty.

"To laugh is to think," observes Georges Bataille.[11] As a general rule, that may be true, especially if we are laughing at ourselves or at the society in which we live. But laughter may also be a refusal to think, especially to think about our responsibilities. To laugh, and to make people laugh at our victims, is the only way to transform our opprobrium and contempt for ourselves into contempt for our victim.[12]

Auschwitz was arrived at a little at a time. The joke about a Jewish suicide was the step that prepared the way for the joke about the direct murder of the Jews. In August, 1933, when the Jew Rosenfelder committed suicide to draw the attention of his Christian friends to the growing anti-Semitic campaign, one newspaper commented: "Fritz Rosenfelder is reasonable, and he hangs himself. We are glad, and we would see nothing wrong with it if his confreres were to say goodbye to us in the same way."[13]

That verifies what we indicated earlier: "Bourgeois coldness" presents itself at first in the guise of smiling detachment. There are those who think that the antidote to smiling detachment is smiling revolution.[14] Such unexpected behavior might take bourgeois coldness by surprise, and cause it to react in a premature and disorderly way, revealing its true nature. But the effect of this antidote, even in those cases where it works, is often fleeting and ephemeral. Worse yet, it can have a negative effect: to force a masquerading mentality such as this one to reveal its true nature before the right time might encourage certain groups to give their open adherence and assent, before the right time, to repressive acts of authoritarian power, thus fostering the intensification of those repressive acts and the consolidation of that authoritarian power.

19

It is from this and similar testimony that the embittered and turbulent political nihilism of today nourishes itself. When all conceivable roads are shown to be closed, the last attempt left is gratuitous violence.

Violence of this kind, violence that is not part of a plan, that has not first established either its objective or the modality for reaching it, is always aleatory. In fact, it is extremely improbable that such action alone can provoke any slide in the power structure.

The attitude of those who commit gratuitous violence is very similar to that of the passionate roulette player. Both have superstitious faith in the *caprice du hasard*; both are contemptuous of calculation. "Sometimes," confesses the gambler Dostoevsky, "some sort of calculation would flash into my head. I would get fond of certain favored numbers and probabilities; but very soon I would abandon them and start betting again almost unconsciously."[15]

This superstition and this contempt, though not always justifiable, are always explainable. We have arrived at today's "post-Auschwitz" in part through the disappointing experience of attempting to make calculation an instrument of liberating violence. Generally, calculation has shown itself to be more amenable to the aims of repressive rather than liberating violence. That is because, at bottom, it is difficult to establish the difference between using calculation in the service of violence, and violence in the service of calculation.[16] This ambiguity has been especially harmful for planning, inasmuch as planning is action that presupposes calculation.

Chapter Four

NEW UTOPIANS

LET US STOP for a moment to consider the planning activities of those whom Robert Boguslaw[1] has called the "new utopians," as distinguished from the "old utopians" of whom we have already spoken, and to whom we shall return later.

There is a big difference between the new and the old utopians. The latter designed models that were prospective abstract structures, and that were hypothetical in terms of the future concrete life of concrete people. On the other hand, the models of the new utopians, though they too constitute prospective abstract structures, try to act on the future (or present) of the abstract life of abstract people—that is to say, of nonpeople. "The new utopians," says Boguslaw, "are concerned with nonpeople, and with people-substitutes. Their planning is done with computer hardware, system procedures, functional analyses, and heuristics. They tend to deal with man only in his workday world without prescribing sex practices, childrearing procedures, or methods for achieving the good life."[2] Following in the footsteps of Saint-Simon and Comte, they maintain that "the administration (or the management, the government) over things must substitute for the administration over persons."[3]

What is really happening today is that men are being transformed into things so that it will be easier to administer them. Instead of working with men, one can work with schemes, numbers, or graphs that represent men.

In that context, models become more important than the objects or the persons of which they are a mere replica.[4] For many years now, the fetishism of models, especially in the fields of economics, politics, and military strategy, has typified the attitude of the late Enlightenment of the modern technocrats.

According to these people, perfection of the instructional and decision-making process is possible only if one succeeds in getting rid of all subjective interference with the construction and manipulation of the models used for obtaining that perfection.[5] Once again, we are faced with the old myth, inspired somehow by neopositivism, postulating an absolute structural identity between the physical world and the social world: Just as it is possible in the physical world to act only on facts and without regard for values, it must also be possible to behave the same way in the social world.

It is an attempt to project a social world without ideologies, without alienation, without any break between subject and object; a world which several philosophers of history have called necessary, but without ever having shown its factual possibility.

Leaving aside for now the approach of those philosophers to this argument, it is obvious that a social world devoid of ideologies, as seen by the modern technocrats, is simply a fiction. That is why Boguslaw, who is himself a "systems engineer," ironically calls his colleagues "new utopians." By trying to avoid ideology, many "systems engineers" violate reality, so that they may fit it into a construct which they *a priori* call a-ideological—and that is a procedure which in fact coincides with the one used by supporters of the most

22

traditional ideological approach. The "false conscience" is usually a construct completely devoid of reality, but which nevertheless continues to pretend to have one.

The spiritual father of the sect of "new utopians" is Robert S. McNamara.[6] During the seven years in which he served as Secretary of Defense, he represented the archetype of the new technocracy, American and international.

A study of the "McNamara case" is of fundamental importance, not least of all because it is the case of a "new utopian" responsible for the concrete exercise of power.[7] His is the story of a tragic misunderstanding, for during his seven years in office, McNamara believed, probably in good faith, that personal dominion over the power of facts was the equivalent of personal dominion over the facts of power.

In his recent book,[8] we get a clear glimpse of the subjective and objective reasons that made the misunderstanding both possible and necessary. At the same time, we can see just as clearly the route that led to the failure of what we have called the ideology of anti-ideology.

From the clamorous rise of McNamara during the Kennedy administration to his rather decorous decline under Lyndon B. Johnson, we can observe the gradual development of a seven-year process that makes any pretense at technocratic rationality seem absurd. McNamara's first public acts, together with his didactic and polemical statements in favor of rationality and against emotionalism—"reason, not emotion"[9]—led people to think that a new era was about to begin in the "administration of things." For the first time, it was said, the vast experience assembled in the "scientific management" of private enterprise could be applied on a much larger scale, in the search for more rational solutions to the great problems of international politics.[10]

We know now that the technocratic intelligentsia did not emerge victorious from that trial. After the "McNamara case," one can well imagine, many dreams evaporated, including the secret dreams of McNamara himself, who surely would never have called himself a dreamer. Certainly his defeat was a hard blow to that feeling of absolute infallibility which up to then had sustained the international technocratic sect, from the "backroom boys" in Washington to the *chozjajstvenniki* in Moscow, not to mention the *anciens élèves* of the École Nationale d'Administration in Paris. It was also a hard blow to all those who, in spite of the nefarious results of Nazi proto-technocracy, continued to nourish the vague hope of building a more humane society through the contribution of the technico-scientific intelligentsia.

That hope is not unjustified in itself; it becomes unjustified because the technico-scientific intelligentsia finds itself forced to act on the basis of arbitrary presuppositions. In other words, the precariousness of McNamara's "basic system" does not derive so much from the type of methodology he uses as from the fragility of the assumptions that serve as its foundation. The fact, for example, that he considers it axiomatic that in our world, all the good is found on one side and all the bad on the other substantially weakens the foundation of his system.[11] In reality, the system is sick even before it is born. Nor can it be healed by an exhaustive, quantitative survey of the facts, or by the use of refined techniques of "systems analysis" and "problem solving." For in fact, those methodological procedures are affected by the general pathology of the very system they are trying to mend.

It is precisely in those areas in which man is the essential element that these methodological procedures cannot ever be absolutely neutral. But in the case of McNamara, we must say that the problem is even more grave than that. Inasmuch as his methodology serves the "administration of things"—or rather, without Saint-Simonian euphemisms, "the administration of men"—it is necessarily a tendentious methodology;

24

but inasmuch as it is part of a Manichean philosophy of history, it is not only tendentious, but also belligerent. It is oriented toward the destruction or annihilation of men who, in its judgment, personify evil. Not accidentally, the result of the "basic system" is the war in Vietnam, the "McNamara war," as it has rightly or wrongly been called.

From what we have said, it emerges that in their first confrontation with the actual reality of power, the instrumental systems of technocracy revealed an obvious operative inadequacy and a clear conceptual vulnerability. This has begun to worry the theoreticians and planners of those systems; many of them have already emphasized the need for a rigorous re-examination of those undeclared or hidden premises, which are impugning the validity of their approach. Their target is the vaunted ideological neutrality of the models they themselves construct.

This new attitude must be explained not only through the "McNamara case" but also through the pressure exerted recently by all sorts of movements of dissent: students, workers, and intellectuals in general. As the economist John Kenneth Galbraith[12] has made clear, the representatives of technical power—that is, technician intellectuals in power—tend to free themselves more and more from entrepreneurial and political power, and very often show a surprising receptivity toward attitudes of social and cultural dissent. "The factory technologists exercise no political function over their instrumental masses," Antonio Gramsci observes acutely, "or at least one can call it a phase already overcome. Sometimes just the contrary takes place, namely that the instrumental masses . . . exercise a political influence on the technicians."[13] And that is precisely what is beginning to take place today everywhere, both in the capitalist and in the socialist countries.

In the German review *Atomzeitalter*, we find the first attempt at a change of front among the theoreticians of "social cybernetics." It is the first attempt, after Boguslaw, to demythicize the preliminary assumptions of its own methodology, and to reintroduce a sociological concern. In the essay *Sozialkybernetik und Herrschaft*, published in that review,[14] Dieter Senghaas discussed this new theme, using the traditional terminology of the school. "This connection clarifies the widespread sophism (*Trugschluss*) that self-regulation, that is to say, self-control, on the one hand and manipulation on the other are identical. Certainly, manipulation is a kind of control (*Steuerung*). But it tends to stupefy. It wobbles (*gaengelt*), whereas self-regulation presupposes autonomy. It invests sums (*Betraege*) in the cultivation (*Erziehung*) of a false conscience (*Bewusstseins*) in individuals, groups, and organizations, whereas cybernetic regulation demands (*erfordert*) self-consciousness. It indoctrinates, without bringing forth (*erzeugen*) a capacity for independent learning. It furthers repression, whereas self-regulatory systems demand emancipation" (page 395). "A policy that makes men stupid becomes stupid itself" (page 398).

Up to this point, we have outlined the past and perhaps a little of the future behavior of the "new utopians." Using the example of McNamara, we have tried to describe first of all their difficulty in overcoming the contrast between program and reality; then, we sought to describe the efforts made recently by several theoreticians of this persuasion to find a greater correspondence between their planned systems and some of the social implications of those systems. Certainly the "new utopians" are now trying to tear free of the vicious cycle of "methodolatry," and to get closer, without betraying their methods, to the theme of Revolution, which at present they prefer to call Emancipation or Social Innovation.

Chapter Five

DESIGN, PLANNING, AND POLITICS

WE BELIEVE IT IS TIME now to re-examine the attitude of those whom we have called the "old utopians," or perhaps better, the "old utopians" of the present day. By present-day "old utopians," we mean principally those planners, especially architects and urban planners, who are formulating ideal models of future cities, which they call "megastructures."[1] We choose to class them as "old utopians" because they have accepted the attitude of traditional utopianism: On the one hand, they refuse to undertake any action that implies a planning compromise with the environmental needs and pressures of the present; and on the other hand, they also refuse to hypothesize any sort of decision-making trajectory that might make these megastructures realizable in the future, and that would enable them to foresee the environmental needs and pressures of which they would eventually become part.

Although we acknowledge that these planners have been very innovative and stimulating, we nevertheless think that they have failed to overcome the contradictions of those who believe in the maieutic force of images and prophetic words alone. The best example is furnished by Buckminster Fuller, whom many "megastructuralists" rightly look upon as their

27

precursor and their inspiration. In his luxuriant and futuristic cosmogony (which, though not always coherent, is nevertheless more productive than the pallid "zoom" literature of his acolytes), the relationship between planning and revolution occupies a place of primary importance.

Buckminster Fuller has spoken frequently of the necessity and possibility of a "Revolution by Design," that is to say, of a Revolution defined in terms of designing and planning. Through the use of designing and planning, it aims at a radical change in the technical structures of exploitation, utilization, and distribution of the natural resources, and at a change in all those other structures of the human environment that are more or less dependent on those resources.

According to Buckminster Fuller, there is enough of everything for everyone on our planet. The frictions of the present day—cold or hot wars, revolutions in the underdeveloped areas —are not so much the result of a dearth of resources as they are of a lack of planning. "When man," he said in a lecture at San Jose State College, "is successful in doing so much more with so much less, that he can take care of everybody at a higher standard, then there will be no fundamental cause for war. In the years ahead, as man does become successful, the root cause of war will be eliminated. Scientists assure us over and over again that this is feasible. There can be enough energy and organized capability for all men to enjoy the whole earth."[2] On another occasion, he suggested moving from the creation of "weaponry" to the creation of "livingry."[3]

In the future, design and planning must assume the responsibility for transforming what is today barely virtual into something real. In that way design and planning would become the guiding factor of the Revolution; in fact, it would itself be the Revolution.

Despite all this, we find ourselves asking what, in this context, are the necessary requisites for changing design into revolution; which are the existing or future power structures that must delegate to the planners the responsibility for radically transforming, in an operation of worldwide dimensions, all the technical structures of the human environment.

Up to now, Buckminster Fuller does not seem to have furnished very precise answers to these questions. Every time he was supposed to make reference to the real context of the Revolution thus conceived, his opinions sounded generally ambiguous, though of course not so ambiguous as to hide his profound conviction.[4]

Evidently, Buckminster Fuller thinks design and planning would resolve the problems that politics has left unsolved for centuries. In other words design and planning would be called in to substitute for politics, to abolish it and cancel it from history. "Politics," he says, "will become obsolete."[5] It is not surprising, then, that he considers the "Revolution by Design" to be exclusively an act of technical imagination: a position typical of technocratic utopianism.

Personally, we accept the principle that the conditions of human existence can be changed through planning, but not in the terms we have just discussed. In our view, the "Revolution by Design" should be the result both of the technical imagination, and of what the sociologist C. Wright Mills called the "sociological imagination"[6]—both technical courage and social and political courage.

A "Revolution by Design" has real meaning only if it is supported by "Design by Revolution." Both, and perhaps the latter more than the former, presuppose the acceptance of an operative political praxis, which means the rejection of political nihilism. But both, and this time perhaps the former more than the latter, presuppose an operative praxis of design, which means the rejection of nihilism in design.

29

Chapter Six

EXPLOSIVE CONGESTION

POLITICALLY SPEAKING, the revolutionary sense of dissent is really only attainable through design. Dissent that rejects hope in design is nothing but a subtle form of consent. Or, if we want to express ourselves more prudently, we can say that dissent devoid of design, dissent with empty hands, is not particularly dangerous to the forces of consent.

The discussion of nondesign is an intellectual luxury of consumer society, a prerogative of well-to-do peoples, the rhetorical pomp of peoples saturated with goods and services. Peoples submerged in indigence and need cannot permit themselves that luxury. For them the will to survive is identical with the will to design, because for them, designing means supplying themselves with the basic weapons against the repressive hostility of indigence. For them designing means conceiving of structures that will allow them on the one hand to maximize the scant resources available, and on the other to minimize the factors that could contribute to the waste of those resources.

We said earlier that in a consumer society, the rejection of hope in planning might seem more an act of consent than of dissent. Strictly speaking, that is only partly true.

As a matter of fact, the complete rejection of *any* form of designing is a double-edged kind of behavior. On the one hand it is certainly an act of open dissent, inasmuch as it repudiates that which in our society continues to pass itself off as the only feasible and valid kind of designing, viz., designing as an activity that seeks to proliferate objects artificially, and then to make their aggregate universe denser and larger, also artificially. But on the other hand, we must also see it as an act of consent to our society, because after all it coincides with the currently prevalent attitude of renunciation—the attitude of abstention and even of outright obstructionism toward a type of designing opposed to the former: that is to say, designing that seeks to open up a horizon of action that is articulated, coherent, and socially responsible for the human environment and its destiny.

The polemical rejection of any form of planning, then, has two aspects: dissent and consent. Let us stop for a moment to consider the second aspect, trying to shed light on this unusual convergence of views between those who protect the established order, and those who would overthrow it.

It is a phenomenon susceptible of many interpretations; but we must say from the start that we are unsatisfied by those that rest upon the insinuation of a "tacit agreement"—that is, on the theory of a basic accord between the radicals of conservation and the radicals of insurrection.

We prefer another interpretation. Although it is neither more subtle nor more probable than the others, it at least has the merit of opening a discussion rich in all kinds of implications. For the sake of exploration, for example, we may hazard the surely indemonstrable assumption that the coincidence alluded to above is not casual, but is rather a tactical (or rather strategic) piece of shrewdness on the part of those seeking a radical change in our society.

According to this conjecture, they understood some time

31

ago that if our society continues to develop as it has up until now—that is, freewheeling, imbued with chaotic spontaneity, with no plan, with no precautions of any sort, and with no environmental designing and planning—it will come to an end very soon, perhaps even sooner than the skeptics predict, and it will end in a catastrophe of the gravest consequences.

In our present environmental surroundings, we can already distinguish the many "time bombs" that threaten the condition of our future lives. We are not referring here to the enormous destructive power of nuclear arms or of missile systems; we are referring rather to the equally enormous destructive power implicit in the uncontrolled development of "populations of all kinds."

By populations, we mean in this context all those functional complexes of homologous entities that may constitute an identifiable and quantifiable class. Such populations may consist not only of persons, but of objects, resources, infrastructures, equipment, processes, messages, cognitions, etc.[1]

The rate of growth of each of these populations already foretells a state of explosive congestion which in the long run will substantially compromise the human environment. Such a statement might well arouse hostile mistrust. At first, it might seem to be one of those many gratuitous prophecies made by the cultivators of a facile Cassandraism, one of the many prognostications made by those visionaries of decline. But this time we must acknowledge that the possibility of an "explosive congestion," with all its attendant harmful effects, is not part of an alarmist rhetoric; on the contrary, it is a real and present danger, to be found everywhere.

Chapter Seven

DISCARDS, RESIDUES, DROSS

By NOW, THE FACTS are public domain; but the general tendency not to recognize their gravity forces us to return to the subject. It is especially necessary when we are faced with the widespread, deceptive, and even hypocritical opinion that the entire problem can be solved by "birth control."

The six billion human beings projected for the year 2000, only thirty years from now, do not represent an isolated problem, as so many latter-day Malthusians would have us believe. The explosive proliferation of our species assumes catastrophic proportions to the extent—and only to the extent—that it takes place together with the even greater proliferation of many other populations. The surface of our earth—what we call *terra firma*—has a total area of about 149 million square kilometers. Of that area, only 63 million square kilometers are habitable by human beings, at least for now. In practice, that area is really far smaller if we consider that in many countries, especially in Greece, Italy, France, Spain, Egypt, Israel, China, Mexico, and Peru, there are vast archaeological areas that cannot be exploited as habitational or as agricultural space. Still, the area optimistically estimated at 63 million square kilometers, even when reduced for archaeological reasons, could host the population foreseen for the year 2000, and even for the year 3000, if we think of the huge alimentary (and perhaps even habitational) possibilities of the sea.

It might be useful to consider in this connection the matter (which has become an obsession) of the relationship between men and vehicles. Naturally that relationship has implications of all kinds, economic, sociological, and even psychiatric; but we often forget that it is first of all a conflictory relationship between two "demographic" universes that have competing interests within one and the same physical environment.

If we estimate the number of human beings and the number of cars produced every second in the United States, and allow living space for each human being and parking space for each car, it turns out that together they "devour" 80 square meters per minute.[1] And this quantification is only partial: in reality, since more cars are born per second than human beings, it is logical that the increase in the area "devoured" is due in the first place to the increase in the number of cars, and only in the second place to the increase in the number of human beings. Nor is that all. In this calculation, we are considering only men and cars, and have excluded all those other populations that take an active part in that banquet at which our earth is "devoured."

Naturally, not all populations appropriate *terra firma* in the same way. Let us take the case of airplanes. They occupy only a limited area and for a brief time; and yet, this particular way of using the earth's surface often causes forms of congestion that are even harder to foresee and control. Not only is the destination airport involved, but the airports of an entire region, all of which must be furnished with a "surplus" of infrastructures and services capable of accommodating rerouted planes. This phenomenon of interlinking congestion takes place with ever-growing frequency, especially in the

United States, and brings about longer waiting lines both on land and in the air. According to Oscar Bakke, Director of the Eastern Region of the Federal Aviation Agency, in 1966 "up to ninety aircraft at a time stand by at Kennedy Airport awaiting clearance for takeoff while as many as thirty others 'hold' to land."[2]

Vehicles and airplanes are visually and symbolically the most obvious objects in the landscape of our technical civilization; but industry also produces vast populations of objects whose presence is perhaps less spectacular, but which are certainly capable of consuming the scant resources of the area around us in a much more homogeneous way. We need only look around to see them: from kitchen machines to machine tools, from furniture to building materials, from clothing to containers, from printed paper to tractors.

There is yet another population not to be underestimated: that which very objectively and sarcastically might be called the population of "waste," that is to say, all the discards, residues, and dross that derive from the life cycle—complete or incomplete—of all the other populations.

If it is true that our society, as we have said, refuses to plan its future environment, it is because society accepts its own capitulation in advance. To assent to this renunciatory attitude —as do many of today's dissenters—is at bottom to contribute to the acceleration of the process of the self-destruction of consumer society.

It is from this point of view that we risked speaking of a tactical—or rather, strategic—piece of shrewdness on the part of the dissenters. Strictly speaking, it amounts to a new version of the old "theory of the collapse" of capitalism.[3] Only this time the collapse would be explained (though not completely) by intrinsic environmental contradictions, and by the design ataraxy that would impede their resolution.

Chapter Eight

DESPERATE HOPE

THE "CONSENTERS" OPPOSE this inevitable "unhappy ending" with their notion of an inevitable "happy ending." Whereas the supporters of the former believe that disengagement from planning will contribute to the collapse of our society, the supporters of the latter maintain that both commitment and noncommitment to planning are at bottom of little importance. At the last moment, on the edge of the abyss, when all seems irretrievably lost, the necessary solutions will come forth, not only to avert the worst, but to open new prospectives toward the best.[1]

Somehow, the supporters of that approach assert, men throughout history have always known how to rise above apparently insurmountable difficulties. Moreover, this century has seen many apocalyptic predictions proved wrong. Although the economic and social contradictions of capitalism that Marx denounced long ago continue to exist, they have undeniably shown themselves to be at least controllable, particularly after Lord Keynes. Moreover, the waste of certain kinds of energy normally utilized in the nineteenth century has not brought about the calamities foreseen by William Stanley Jevons but, on the contrary—and at the last moment

36

indeed—has led to the discovery of new resources of energy.

But even if the apocalyptic forecasts have not come true, we ought not to feel authorized to discard summarily and on principle all of the negative predictions made about our future. Some new facts counsel greater caution.

In the last decades, the three basic components of our biotic system—air, water, and earth—have been mistreated atrociously, to the point where in many areas of our planet, especially in the great industrial and urban center, we can already see a substantial (and irreversible, irreparable) rupture in the ecological equilibrium.[2] It means, in effect, that in the long run human beings will not be able to inhabit those portions of our earth.

This grave problem is further complicated by the fact that those critical areas are expanding at a rapid rate. Faced with that reality, the future cannot help but look worrisome, even to the most optimistic.

We must now recognize that it is pointless to oppose positive predictions to negative predictions; and pointless too is the ambiguous do-nothingism implicit in the theory of the "happy ending." No technological triumph, whether astronautical or what have you, can serve as an alibi for rejecting the evidence of these "new facts."

Here we must ask ourselves, What road led to this environmental situation? What factors contributed to this threat to the health of the components of our biotic system?

In a general way, we have already answered these questions. If we look closely, we see that the phenomenon is produced by the uncontrolled increase in human and nonhuman populations of all sorts, all in conflict, forming a web of contrasting needs that becomes ever more delicate, vast, and complex.

Still, we must admit that this explanation, though valid, is too generic. We must point out specifically that there are at least two populations which, in our opinion, are the most

37

directly responsible for the ecological impoverishment just denounced. They are two populations joined by a causal nexus. One we have christened the "population of waste," and the other is the "population of pollutants and artificial factors of erosion." The relationship between them is at once patent and hidden, brutal and subtle; and its logical development has the same linearity as the process of which it is the expression.

It is the process that is unleashed every time the decision is made to abolish an industrial product. From that moment, the segregated product must not only desert the market, but must also physically disappear.[3]

Suddenly, through an arbitrary *Diktat*, a hitherto desirable product becomes undesirable, one item more in the vast "population of waste." But the item, by no means docile, shows an energetic will to survive; in most cases, it stubbornly resists every violence perpetrated upon it to annihilate it.

It is not easy to make a "clean slate" in the world of objects. It seems to be easier to produce an object than to make it disappear. Even the most highly refined technical tricks are only of limited help. One can try to reduce the object's dimensions, compress it, fragment it, reuse it, or recuperate it partially as raw material; but despite all this, some cumbrous residue always remains. Then, after many complicated operations, actions, and manipulations, when we think we are finally finished, we recognize that the object has only apparently abdicated its materiality; there was only a tactical retreat from the tangible to the intangible, from the mechanical world to the chemical world.

The object has lost its morphological identity, and is no longer recognizable; it no longer belongs to the "population of waste," of degraded objects. It has passed over to become part of another population. After a drastic transformation, the ingredients of the object have become part of the "population of pollutants and artificial factors of erosion."

38

As distinguished from the other, this population does not "occupy" habitable space, but rather contaminates, corrodes, debases, dissolves, and withers it. In the end, it renders the space uninhabitable by human beings.

It is therefore chimerical of those tacticians of the collapse of capitalism ("the worse it gets—the better") to believe that the enormous destructive potentialities of these "time bombs" can be restricted to a specific geographical area or to a particular type of society.

The truth is that if energetic countermeasures are not taken in time, our maltreatment of the environment might well compromise, in the opinion of students of ecology, the destiny of every form of human life on the surface of the earth, perhaps even by the second half of the coming century.

There are those who maintain that such a gloomy future is no less desirable than any other. Everything, they warn us, is destined to end sooner or later. It makes no fundamental difference whether we resign ourselves to accept a certain end in the short run, or make a desperate attempt to postpone that end as long as possible. Although it is extremely obvious, we can recognize the validity of this thesis; but precisely because there is no fundamental difference between the one attitude and the other, each man is free to make the choice he deems more proper, more suitable to his convictions.

It is a choice between destructive pessimism and constructive pessimism. We in fact prefer the latter. For us, there exists only one possibility: to keep rejecting everything that threatens human survival; to help defuse the "time bomb," which means to respond to irresponsible growth with responsible control, to respond to congestion with management. In brief, we choose design and planning.

Chapter Nine

REALITY OF MESOCOSMOS

Is THERE STILL ROOM for design and planning? Frankly, the opportunity is greatly reduced. The very high complexity of environmental problems obliges us to try to solve them technically; and we have already seen, when discussing Buckminster Fuller's approach, to what degree of abstraction technological imagination can lead when its infinite possibilities are given free play—especially when it functions without the aid of the sociological imagination.

The recent loudly acclaimed successes of the space capsules, culminating in the landing of the first man on the moon, have once again given currency to hope in the possibility of making the human environment absolutely artificial.[1]

Though the idea seems seductive at first sight, it cannot be accepted hastily or entirely. The questions it leaves unanswered are too important and too numerous. Many scientists, in fact, have already expressed doubts about solutions of that kind. Obviously, the human capacity for adaptation, though immense, is not infinite. Not long ago the biologist Adolphe Portmann[2] reminded us that the specific human environment, biologically speaking, is neither the macrocosm nor the microcosm, but the mesocosm constituted by the *oikos*, the hearth of man. For phylogenetic and ontogenetic reasons, man is condemned to remain in the mesocosm. Of course man can undertake temporary voyages toward the macrocosm as he is now doing, but he must always take with him his artificial mesocosm.

In the next few decades, there will quite probably no longer be any obstacles—at least from a technical point of view—to an absolute artificialization of the human mesocosm, in a part or in the whole of our planet. But even in the coming decades, it will not be known—not even theoretically—whether man can survive in the long run if forced to live forever in an artificial mesocosm. In fact, we have reason to doubt that anyone can seriously guarantee, in the near future, that men living under such conditions would not be subjected to substantial degenerative processes in their neuro-vegetive and homeostatic systems.[3]

At times we suspect that these speculations on the future of the human environment are meant to mask a certain amount of technocratic evasiveness. It would seem that these speculations are being used to avoid the more difficult and urgent task of obtaining here and now a new type of mesocosm, of the kind proposed by Patrick Geddes,[4] in which there will take place an "optimization" not only of the environment but also, and above all, of man as an individual and social being. Naturally there are those who consider this suspicion absolutely unfounded. These men assure us that the changes being wrought today in our habitat by science and technology will also bring with them essential changes in the human condition.

Indeed, the advent of a new human condition is supposed to be imminent. Its early forms are already discernible in the metropolitan and megalopolitan agglomerates of the highly industrialized nations. This phenomenon, it is suggested, invalidates the suspicion of (or objection to) the one-sidedness of technocracy, and its evasive indifference toward the social environment.

41

Chapter Ten

LABYRINTH OF COMPLEXITY

RECENT TIMES HAVE WITNESSED an outpouring of literary and philosophical portrayals of the future human condition with new and ever more provocative peculiarities attributed to it every day. At one time, posthistoric man is announced, at another, postideological man; and finally we have postalphabetical man.[1] The inevitable prefix "post" in these and similar characterizations always indicates the intention of a radical break with the past. What is being attacked is the traditional human condition, or better, the traditional conditioning of man, as it has developed for at least the last two thousand years. I refer precisely to historical, ideological, and alphabetized man, who after all constituted the grand design and the grand accomplishment of our culture. On a very abstract level, there is really no objection to an attempt of that kind. But on a more concrete level, and with greater regard for practical consequences, we find that serious guarantees are lacking in this case too.

It is certain that up to now, despite the valid conceptual contributions of several scholars in this field,[2] we have surely not yet succeeded in establishing the limit to which it is possible to change the human condition without running the risk of altering and even annihilating human nature. Until this has been done adequately, the attempt to alter the human condition radically shall continue to be, in our judgment, a "leap into the void."

And yet today, perhaps more than ever before, nothing stops us, at least subjectively, from making these "leaps into the void." Any adventure is sure to find convinced participants, any proposal, even the most poorly founded, seems capable of realization to its supporters. It is true that constraints do exist, as they always have; but they are so many, so varied, and so contradictory, that in the end they do not really function as constraints; nor does anyone consider them such.

For the first time we are living the illusion of absolute impunity; for the first time, we believe we can unleash actions without caring about their possible consequences. There is much talk about innovation (and even more about revolution), but no one cares to know what real risks accompany them. No one seems willing to recognize that innovative behavior in any field is an act of management, directed toward keeping the risk under control and measuring its consequences. "The process of decision-making associated with innovation," observes Donald A. Schon, "is a process of risk-reduction. . . . The innovative work . . . consists in converting uncertainty to risk."[3] Here, innovative action and design are very similar. Both work at the same front; that is, they try to find the probabilities of risk implicit in every uncertainty, and to identify the "maximum credible risk."

At bottom, we are dealing with the same behavior, which can generically be called innovative design. Still, if we want to be more rigorous, we must admit that planning is always directed toward a critical assessment of the problem it faces, whereas the same is not always true of innovation. That is to say, there are some kinds of innovation, few, to be sure, that do not derive from design. On the other hand, we must also

43

note that planning, even with all its observation and decision-making, only rarely succeeds in becoming innovation. To sum up, design innovation and nondesigned innovation are equally infrequent.

These nuances may seem superfluous, but they have the precise aim of placing definite limits to our notion of innovative designing. Thus we avoid, it seems to us, the vain temptation of imagining that innovative design is the "real way" that leads inevitably to innovation, and that it offers an absolute guarantee against any arbitrary surprise.[4]

Since the arguments we are now presenting deal mainly with problems inherent in the human environment, all our remarks, be they on design or on innovation, are centered around that particular family of problems which experts in heuristic and decision-making techniques call "ill-defined problems."[5]

Those are precisely the problems most difficult to pose and to solve. Usually, the system of which man is a part presents "ill-defined problems," or, as Warren Weaver called them, "problems of disorganized complexity."[6] For a better understanding of the nature of such a system, Weaver suggests that we imagine them as "a large billiard table with millions of balls rolling over its surface." In other words, it is a system of very high unpredictability, inasmuch as all its components are forced to behave in a way that is at once highly dynamogenetic and erratic.

The space capsule, inasmuch as it is an artificial environment, has vast innovative meaning mainly because it transformed a system of ill-defined problems—that is, of disorganized complexity—into a system of well-defined problems —that is, of organized complexities.

Still, it is obvious that this formidable success is possible only because of the small dimensions of the system in question. Were we to try to broaden it to a planetary scale, we should find ourselves once again on Weaver's "large billiard table." And there, we should have to attempt an infallible prediction of the risk, which implies foreseeing the trajectory of all those variables whose behavior in such a system is dynamogenetic and erratic. In the present state of our knowledge, that would be an exercise in futility.

Chapter Eleven

DEURBANIZATION AND
DESOCIALIZATION

On the basis of such evidence, we begin to see clearly that the idea of planning a totally artificial perfection of the human environment can only have the value of a "trial balloon." It is a speculative construct likely to verify precisely the non-plausibility of the idea itself.

It must be remembered, however, that planners have other proposals which, though very similar to the preceding one in their foundations, are very different in their objectives, which are much more circumscribed. These are the proposals that seek to perfect our ecosystem not in entirety, but in part; they do not, in other words, take on the enormous task of working on our entire planet, but rather only on a particular city or region.

These can really be called attempts at "suboptimization."[1] Buckminster Fuller's "Dome Over Manhattan," an immense translucent bell that covers the entire midtown area of New York,[2] is typical of a proposal for suboptimization. But the fact that such a proposal is technically feasible today tells us nothing, absolutely nothing, about the ecology of the "habitat" that would develop under such a supposedly protective cupola. In this connection, we are not pacified by the assurances that such an environment would be completely air-conditioned, and that its inhabitants would enjoy the delights of absolute meteorological neutrality. The idea demonstrates once again the admirable imagination of Buckminster Fuller as an engineer, but it also shows his dangerous ingenuity as an extemporaneous ecologist.

Aside from this sort of suboptimization based on the attempt to artificialize the environment partially, there is another that proceeds from different presuppositions. It is the suboptimization advanced by the "systems engineers" involved in aerospace research.

Their approach consists above all in a design for the radical redistribution of the functional and structural "tasks" within a particular area. The most interesting study illustrative of this direction is the one done by systems engineers for the renewal of environmental conditions in California.

In 1964 the governor of California, Edmund G. Brown, made the following announcement: "We decided to test the theory that systems engineers, who could move astronauts around the globe in 90 minutes, could move a father to and from work a little faster or sweep away enough smog to give us a clear look at the sky."[3]

Contrary to what we might have expected, systems engineers from industry and space research did not respond to this challenge by proposing a "capsule" around California. Their response was quite measured, and generally did not go beyond the more conventional ideas of American experts in "urban renewal."

Only on a few points do their arguments take on a more polemical character. It is particularly evident in their proposal for reversing the relationship between the worker and work, with the suggestion that work be brought to the worker, instead of the other way around. At first, the proposal does not seem very original, or at least not very different from the rather

47

widespread tendency to place industrial plants outside (or even very far from) urban centers, closer to cheaper energy and human resources.

But the systems engineers are proposing something quite different. First of all, in designing such a model, they were not concerned with workers in general, but rather specifically with white-collar workers. Moreover, their proposal would not bring offices closer to the employees, but rather put the office work into their homes. It would mean nothing less than splitting up office work into as many parts as there are employees' homes. Thus, the home of the employee would be transformed into a "domicile office," into a small work unit perfectly equipped with technical means of communication, calculation, and programming, so that the employee could do all his office tasks at home. He would be able to do any kind of work that requires the elaboration and management of information: receiving, listing, verifying, evaluating, deciphering, interpreting, storing, and producing and transmitting messages.

Systems engineers think they can thereby remove from the city a large number of office workers; and these, as everyone knows, constitute the fixed or commuting part of the population whose rate of growth is the highest among all those that are causing the congestion in the great urban agglomerates of today.

In contradistinction to other models of technical utopianism, this one describes in rather precise detail the nature and functioning of the necessary technical apparatus.

Here again, there are no technical obstacles to the realization of the proposal. But if the technological inspiration behind the "Dome Over Manhattan" leads us to an ecological aberration, the model developed for California brings us to a sociological aberration. In fact, the removal of workers from their places of collective work cannot be seen as a positive fact. Today it may be only a question of white-collar workers; but tomorrow, all other workers might be included. Making work a private matter will be the beginning of deurbanization, and in the end will bring the desocialization of man. Mass man, we all know, is manipulable; but isolated man is even more so.[4]

Chapter Twelve

THE IDEA OF SYSTEM

IF WE ACCEPT THE SORT of designing that is devoid of a lucid critical consciousness (both ecological and social), we will always be led to evade contingent reality.

In the final analysis, that sort of designing is only a disguised form of antidesign. Obviously the keen taste for the "leap into the void" is typical of antidesign. Still, we find this taste as prevalent among the technical utopians as among the millenarian utopians. In the former, paradoxically, it comes as a result of a hypertrophy of interest in planning; in the latter, it is an atrophy of that interest. Both tendencies agree in not wanting to translate their will to action into terms of concrete and immediate management.

As we have already seen, there can be design without innovation, and innovative activity without planning. But neither planning nor innovation can do without the service of management. As soon as there is something to design or innovate, the discussion concerning it can only be carried out in the framework of the factual world to which it refers. In other words, the discussion must deal with management of the facts that are to be designed or innovated. And finally, it must be a discussion of *negotium gestio*, of responsibility (directly assumed or delegated) for a specific piece of reality.

Let us now try to examine the concept of management thoroughly. In current political and trade-union discussion, we often hear the concept of management opposed by the concept of self-management. This has led to the notion that self-management is the sort of management that succeeds in being nonrepressive by ceasing to be management. That is a grave logical distortion.

Let us define first of all what we mean by management. In our opinion, management is the operative and cognitive behavior by means of which information is transformed into action. Like all processes, therefore, it cannot help but be conditioned by the world within which and as a function of which it acts. This does not necessarily mean that management is behavior that is in accord with its world; there are examples of management (and not always self-management) that overtly or covertly try to subvert its world.

These principles are diametrically opposed to those maintained by intransigent exponents of the current youth rebellion. According to them, all management is necessarily in accord with the world in which it acts. Furthermore, they say, those who do the managing in such a world are always the servile attendants of what they call "the system." In the jargon of protest, system is a word of extreme semantic weakness. We must examine it more closely.

What does system mean in this context? What does it mean to be the servile attendants of a system? Is it even possible for an individual or a group to be completely outside any system? We must admit that such questions are not easy to answer. Nothing that the philosophy of science has recently taught us about the notion of system can help us to justify the way the term is now being used in all quarters.

Sometimes we get the impression that the word "system" is now being used the way the word "regime" was once used. It seems to allude generally to the social status quo—that is to say, to the totality of formal and informal power structures

51

that govern society. The radicals' identification of the concept of system with the concept of power often leads them to assume that opposition to a given "status quo" of power will automatically liberate them from all system.

It is once again the myth that Nicolai Hartmann,[1] in a philosophical context, called "aporetism"; that is, the illusion of being free of all system in thought and action. It is once again the myth of the pure spectator, the incorruptible legislator Utopus, who is able to judge everything "from the outside" because he is neither a user nor a usufructuary of the system.

The concept of system as developed by the philosophy of science absolutely excludes the possibility of the existence of any element that does not fit into some system. The earliest attempts to formulate a "general theory of systems" were made by the biologist Ludwig von Bertalanffy.[2] Indeed, he was the first to essay a precise description of the two fundamental classes of systems, closed and open.

According to von Bertalanffy, all biosystems ("living-systems") are open systems—and that includes social systems, which are "biosystems" too. But social systems have a peculiar nature: One can leave them only to enter into another system. It is just not possible to satisfy the paradoxical desire to get out of a system and yet remain within it. Within any network of interrelations, a man may choose one circuit rather than another; but no one can refuse all the circuits without accepting a change of network—that is to say, a change of system.[3]

This basic bipolarization defined by von Bertalanffy was later enriched by the contributions of C. Foster, Anatol Rapoport, and E. Trucco, who established the existence of three (not two) classes of systems: isolated systems (where neither matter nor energy can be exchanged between the system and the environment); closed systems (where energy but not matter can be exchanged); and open systems (where both matter and energy can be exchanged).[4]

According to this typology, social systems, like all other biosystems, are normally open (as has already been emphasized); but in certain exceptional cases they show a tendency to become closed and even isolated. That is clearly observable in coercive and authoritarian social systems of the past and present. Moreover, historical experience has demonstrated that the most closed or most isolated social systems (or at least those that seem so) are usually the most fragile. Their lack of elasticity (and consequent lack of adaptability) renders them particularly vulnerable to the influence of endogenous and exogenous factors of deviation.

Chapter Thirteen

REVOLUTION AND
STRATEGY OF INNOVATION

It is not at all surprising, then, that many scholars have tried to explain social systems in terms of mechanics, and especially in terms of dynamic equilibrium. One of the first to move in this direction was Vilfredo Pareto,[1] though the idea of system as a "configuration in equilibrium" was probably born long ago with Condillac, who defined system as "an order in which all the parts mutually sustain each other."[2] The idea of system furnished by Condillac, completed by the mechanistic contribution of Pareto, constitutes the basis of one of the best-known schools of American sociology, the school of Talcott Parsons.[3]

In his theory of social system, Parsons says it is impossible for factors of deviation to transmute a given social system into another. He considers deviation a pathological reality, to be combated or rendered innocuous by means of more or less subtle acts of socialization or acculturation.

Recently A. D. Hall, a "systems engineer," tried to elaborate a notion of system completely independent of the traditional notion of equilibrium.[4] Hall considers the dynamics of systems, which he calls "progressive factorization," to be a process that unfolds in the two opposite directions of "decay" and

54

"growth."[5] With that, Hall neutralizes the foundation of the problem; but he does not make clear which agents within the system lead to "decay," and which lead to "growth."

The sociologist Walter Buckley, on the other hand, takes a more precise position on this matter.[6] In every social system, he observes, we can identify two processes, the "morphostatic" and the "morphogenetic." The first preserves, whereas the second innovates; the first conserves the form, organization, and state of the system, whereas the second contributes to its change. Furthermore, in contrast to the out-and-out conservatism of Parsons' school, Buckley maintains that under exceptionally favorable circumstances, a morphogenetic process can transform one system into another; that is, it can contribute to the substitution of one system by another.

The problem of the function, location, and application of morphogenetic factors in a given social system corresponds basically to the questions of how, when, and where innovative factors and even social revolution can make headway and be successful. Modern systematology, as we have seen, seems to furnish very convincing answers to such questions.

There is no doubt that morphogenetic processes usually begin as phenomena of deviation or break from established sociocultural values; but their final success depends on the degree of skill with which they are handled. In fact, there is no possibility of innovation and even less of revolution if the morphogenetic process does not begin with (or soon introduce) a discussion of the technicity of plan, design, and management of the process itself. The history of the many unsuccessful and the few successful revolutions demonstrates that. In general, we can say that if the degree of technicity governing the morphostatic processes is greater than that governing the morphogenetic processes, the possibilities of success will be rather minimal for the latter.

We can see this very clearly if we study the interrelationships within social systems that have attained a very high structural and functional complexity, as is the case in the highly developed countries, both capitalist and socialist. It is less clear in the case of the relatively simple systems in certain primitive cultures, like some of the communities of Indians in North America. In these communities, in fact, a revolt against a universally accepted "totem" may suffice to unleash a morphogenetic process that the morphostatic processes will find hard to control. It might be enough, for example, to start a discussion of totemic innovation by proposing "a Strawberry Order of the Tobacco Society where before there had been a Snowbird Order."[7]

But these small, simple communities are slowly disappearing. More and more, the social systems of the future will be of the type we defined earlier as systems of very high structural and functional complexity. In them, a symbolic (or rather, emblematic) revolt can, to be sure, unleash a morphogenetic process; but it can never of itself assure the success of that process. The morphostatic technicity of these systems is such that every symbolic deviation can be neutralized in the long run. The most frequent procedure, after all, is not very different from the old and still very effective British practice of offering the title of lord to a person who becomes too difficult for the lords.

Chapter Fourteen

SPONTANEOUS ACTION AND POWER

OBVIOUSLY, BUCKLEY'S APPROACH opens new prospects for the analysis of the phenomenon of revolution, not so much because of his conclusions as for the novelty of his insights. His contribution is exclusively in method; his conclusions, in fact, are not substantially new. Earlier students of the phenomenon, using different insights, arrived at similar conclusions. Still, if we want to evaluate his contribution more precisely, we can best do it by a thorough examination of the polemic that has arisen among the various scholars, and led each to conclusions that are not always the same.

To that end we can analyze the old debate, still pertinent today, on how revolutions are made, that is to say, on the nature of innovative processes in society. In particular, we can take a close look at the position held by Hannah Arendt, who considers the constant of all modern revolutions to be spontaneous action, action without plans, without programs, and without models. "The role of the professional revolutionary," she writes, "is of great importance in all modern revolutions; but the role is not played in the preparation of armed or unarmed revolts. . . . The outbreak of most revolutions came as a surprise to the professional revolutionaries and to the parties of the left, just as it did to everyone else; and there is no revolution, not even the Chinese, which is really attributable to them. . . . The purpose of the professional revolutionaries then, is not to make revolutions, but to take power once they have broken out."[1]

If that interpretation is correct, it would follow that the professional "planners" of social innovation, the *Berufsrevolutionäre*, are the ultimate beneficiaries of the innovation, not its authors. The planners are not those who unleash the process of social change, but only those who guide the process that follows after the change has taken place. According to this viewpoint, a revolution can be made without any preceding plans, but would then require plans to stabilize and consolidate itself.

Obviously, the anarchists have always found it easier to accept the first rather than the second part of this argument. For them, as for the professional revolutionary Rosa Luxemburg,[2] the passage from the destruction of an old order to the construction of a new order was always viewed as the passage from a revolutionary to a counterrevolutionary phase. Everything that happens after the revolution must always and in every case be counterrevolutionary. To be sure, if we define revolution only in terms of spontaneous action, everything that is not spontaneous must be discarded as counterrevolutionary. One can see that the argument does not lack a logic of its own.

No one can deny that the construction of any order presupposes the development of a coherent, articulated, and above all centralized structure; in other words, it implies accepting the restoration of a power. And at this point we must not forget that just as innovation is always *against* someone, so too must the installation of a power always take place *against* someone. Despite all the attempts made in these last decades to define more clearly the notion of power (or authority), the

58

definition offered by Max Weber, perhaps because of its impartial cynicism, continues to be the closest to reality: "Power, that is, the possibility of getting obedience to a given command."[3] Weber has harsh words for those who believe in the possibility of social innovation without planning or without the necessary organizing structures—that is to say, without any sort of "apparatus." "Anyone who wants to establish absolute justice on earth by force will need followers; he will need a human 'apparatus.' "[4]

In all ages, the *révoltés* (Anabaptists, millenarians, mystics, anarchists, etc.) have rejected any attempt to instrumentalize men as functions of power; in other words, they have refused to make men become components in an "apparatus." Basically, they were interested in being expressive, not operative, in history; they favored deeds, not plans. But the vulnerable point of the *révoltés* is precisely the one attributed to Thomas Münzer, one of the most illustrious precursors of modern revolution:[5] They love the revolt more than the world to which it could give birth. The *révoltés* are generally criticized for wanting only to aestheticize politics;[6] for the detoxicating pleasure of a *tragischer Monat* (Münster, 1932), of a *semana trágica* (Barcelona, 1909), or of a *semaine de Mai* (Paris, 1968), they are ready to compromise an action that is surely less turbulent but probably more effective.

59

Chapter Fifteen

LAS VEGAS AND
THE SEMIOLOGICAL ABUSE

WE HAVE ALREADY POINTED OUT that not all forms of cultural nihilism must necessarily be considered expressions of a will to dissent from an established social order. There is also a kind of cultural nihilism which, consciously or unconsciously, exalts the status quo. We find an example of it among those who are singing paeans to the "landscape" of certain American cities, which are among the most brutal, degrading, and corrupt that consumer society has ever created.

The city of Las Vegas is usually chosen for these exercises in conformist gymnastics. Interest in the phenomenon of Las Vegas is certainly not new; but in recent years, it has regained currency through the literary activity of a group of writers, journalists, critics, artists, and architects, all of them trying to present this city as the most salient environmental creation of the popular culture of our day.

Tom Wolfe is among those who have done the most to diffuse that idea. And the success of his effort is due in no small measure to the experimental freshness of the language he uses to describe the "landscape" of Las Vegas. In his book *The Kandy-Kolored Tangerine-Flake Streamline Baby,*[1] we read: "Las Vegas has succeeded in wiring an entire city with this network of electronic stimulation, day and night, out in the middle of the desert . . . [page 7]. Las Vegas is the only town in the world whose skyline is made up neither of buildings, like New York, nor of trees, like Wilbraham, Massachusetts, but signs. One can look at Las Vegas from a mile away on Route 91, and see no buildings, no trees, only signs. But what signs! They tower. They revolve, they oscillate, they soar in shapes before which the existing vocabulary of art history is helpless . . . [page 8]. In the Young Electric Sign Company era, signs have become the architecture of Las Vegas, and the most whimsical Yale-seminar-frenzied devices of the two late geniuses of Baroque Modern, Frank Lloyd Wright and Eero Saarinen, seem rather stuffy business, like a jest at a faculty meeting, compared to it [page 9]."

These provocative remarks by Tom Wolfe were taken up and subtly developed by the American architect Robert Venturi, who is in fact a professor at Yale. He too starts out with a lucid analysis of the environmental reality of Las Vegas, and goes on to sketch a general theory of urban perception. For Venturi, Las Vegas is an "existing landscape" from which architects and urban planners have much to learn. He offers Las Vegas as the best available model by which to verify (empirically, so to speak) certain old and new theories of the city as a "fact of communication," as a system of signs.

We must acknowledge that in a general sense, the assessment is not without foundation. Obviously Las Vegas is the first city for which speaking of signs does not presuppose too sophisticated a semiotic set of ideas—a set of ideas, by the way, that has never been very convincingly established.[2] In the case of Las Vegas, a "sign" is not a street, a staircase, a door, a window, or some particular articulation between external and internal space. There, "signs" refer almost exclusively to those gigantic neon signs, or to those equally gigantic iconic emblems. In an article on Las Vegas,[3] written in collaboration with D. Scott Brown, Venturi observes: "The graphic sign in space has become the architecture of this landscape . . . [page 38]. Symbol dominates space. Architecture is not enough. Because the spatial relationships are made by symbols more than by forms, architecture in this landscape becomes symbol in space, rather than form in space . . . the building is the sign [page 39]."

But Venturi is not mainly concerned with furnishing an exceptionally significant (and therefore legible) model capable of meeting the requirements of a rigorous semiotic analysis of urban structures. His is the polemical aim of showing the opposed results of two different "methods of forming" these structures. On the one hand, there is the city made by a *Diktat* of the urban planners, the true exponents of "enlightened despotism" of this era: a city whose physiognomy is established once and for all time by a series of formal and functional choices of an absolutely *a priori* nature; and on the other hand, there is the city which, like Las Vegas, develops out of the dynamic spontaneity of popular expression, and in response to the constantly renewed needs of communicative environmental consumerism.

Once again, we find ourselves faced with the opposition that Banham had perceived: "Few, but roses" and "many, but orchids"—a phrase we subjected to critical commentary some ten years ago.[4] It is the contrast between a "way of forming" that is Platonic, absolutistic, with pretensions toward permanence—a "fine art" way; and a "way of forming" that is realistic, possibilistic, transitory—a "popular art" way.

Still, it would be unjust to say that Venturi (like Banham before him in the field of "industrial design") is content merely with denouncing the conflict between these two different approaches to the urban phenomenon, or will merely declare, as Banham did, that his sympathies were with "popular art." Venturi goes further. His intention, though he does not declare it explicitly, is to hypothesize a middle way between these two tendencies. His proposal seems quite clear. The "fine art" way of forming a city should appropriate the perceptive strategy of the "popular art" way.[5] That is what Venturi means by "learning from Las Vegas." The operation would consist in transmuting the factors of disordered complexity, which are inevitable in urban agglomerates and are normally considered harmful, into factors of creative visual ambiguity, precisely in the sense exemplified by the paintings of Josef Albers.

This idea was taken up by the architect Amos Rapoport and the psychologist Robert E. Kantor, who used it to develop a very ambitious theory of the functional role of ambiguity in environmental perception. "We may visualize," they write, "a range of perceptual input from sensory deprivation (monotony) to sensory satiation (chaos). In the case of the former, there is not enough to observe, to select, to organize; there is an excess of order. In the latter, there is too much to observe, there is no relation between the elements, so that one is overwhelmed by multiplicity."[6] In accord with Venturi, they propose an architecture that is equidistant from "deprivation" and "satiation"—an architecture of ambiguity.

Up to this point everything would be clear and even quite convincing if the authors did not look upon ambiguity only as the factor that impedes "deprivation," and never as the factor which, beyond a certain critical threshold, can in fact lead to "deprivation."

Recent psychological research on curiosity has established experimentally that "deprivation" and "satiation" do not constitute two sealed-off compartments, two opposed and isolated realities; on the contrary, they are two moments of one and the same process of perception.[7] Sarah Bernhardt's famous living room, despite its multiplicity of all kinds of stimuli, is more an example of "deprivation" than of "satiation"—or, to

63

be more exact, the "satiation" is such that it becomes "deprivation." In other words boredom, "the nostalgia for a content," as Marx defines it,[8] is just as present in the immobility that accompanies a scarcity of images as it is in the tumult of their superabundance.

For Las Vegas, as for all our cities, the great problem is not the danger of reaching "deprivation" because of a *lack* of stimuli but rather because of their excess. Contrary to what Venturi thinks, after a certain point "more *is* less." In view of that, it is inconceivable that he should insist on the constant addition of new stimuli and the creation of new phenomena of ambiguity.

This argument is connected with an equally important agrument. In his zeal to refute the formalism of those whom he vaguely calls the "orthodox modern architects," Venturi finds in Las Vegas a "richness of meaning" that he ostentatiously prefers to the "clarity of meaning" of those architects.[9] It is not out of cultural puritanism, but because of our abiding faith in critical consciousness that we simply cannot accept Las Vegas as an example of "richness of meaning." On the contrary: In our opinion, Las Vegas shows just what depths of communicative poverty can be reached by a city left to its own arbitrary development, responsive only to the needs of those builders of "signs," to the needs of casino and motel owners, and to the needs of real estate speculators.

The ambiguity so dear to Venturi is completely lacking in this orgiastic proliferation of "signs." Each "sign" is a stereotyped, crystallized message, a semantic vehicle whose connection to what it claims to design, denote, or signify is never made clear. The result is an epidermal communication, devoid of density and depth. It is fictitious communication, a simulacrum of communication, just chit-chat, just "noise."[10]

Coleridge said that "all languages perfect themselves by a gradual process of desynonymizing words originally equivalent."[11] This definition was formulated more than a century and a half ago not by a linguist but by a poet, and it is one of the most exact definitions of the creative role of ambiguity in the dynamics of language.

In Las Vegas, the process of desynonymization never takes place. It is a city of "signs," but of unequivocal "signs"; there is no possibility of interpreting them in any but one way. The reason is that such signs, at bottom, are not alive, but mummified; they are sign-emblems that serve only as stimulating décor to the pseudocommunicative farce of the age in which we live.

Venturi, and with him many supporters of pop art, are open to criticism for their conformism, and for their lack of historical perception and critical capacity in their dealings with the products of the culture industry of our society.[12] Venturi assures us: "Las Vegas is being analyzed here only as a phenomenon of architectural design; its values are not questioned." With that, he is trying not to identify himself with the object he describes, but he is not very convincing. There is in fact every reason to suppose, without being terribly unfair, that Venturi believes in Las Vegas. In his article he often manages to make us understand not only that he is not troubled by this dazzling jungle of signs, but on the contrary that he considers it a revolutionary turn in the environmental history of man. He considers Las Vegas the result of an authentic outburst of popular fantasy. And there he is mistaken. Las Vegas is not a creation *by* the people, but *for* the people.[13] It is the final product—one might even call it almost perfect of its kind—of more than half a century of masked manipulatory violence, directed toward the formation of an apparently free and playful urban environment, like a Luna Park. But it is an environment in which men are completely devoid of innovative will and of resistance to the effects of the pseudocommunicative intoxication mentioned earlier.

As for the disorder in Las Vegas, Venturi does not consider

it such. Calling Bergson to his aid, he defines disorder as "an order which we cannot see." Clearly, if the dichotomy order-disorder can be the object of abstract metaphysical speculation (as it was for Aristotle, Saint Augustine, Saint Thomas, Spinoza, and surely also for Bergson), it is an even more real and contingent subject from an operative-existential point of view. Undoubtedly, for example, the current disorder in traffic everywhere might well conceal a subtle "vital order" à la Bergson; but for those of us who suffer the physical and psychological effects of that disorder, it is difficult to imagine any sort of order behind it, vital or otherwise.

Venturi, very much like Kevin Lynch, seems to be interested solely in the visual aspects of the city, in the city as "landscape"; the value of a city as an "operative-existential territory" is either forgotten, underestimated, or deferred. He has a definite tendency to function always as a spectator, rarely as an actor in the city. And if Bergson can be of assistance to a spectator, he cannot help an actor.

For the actor, for the man who sees himself operating and living in a city, the only thing that can help is a more scientific foundation of the dichotomy order-disorder. This dichotomy has long been studied and debated in the philosophy of science. The bipolarization order-disorder is inseparable from the bipolarization simplicity-complication.[14] Obviously, environmental design and planning must have the task of making order; its function is ever that of bringing ordered complexity back to systems which are always and by their very nature tending toward disordered complexity—that is, toward complication.

Chapter Sixteen

TOWARD A PRAXIOLOGY OF DESIGN

THE OPEN ENTHUSIASM for Las Vegas (and for similar "existing landscapes") can be explained as a polemical rejection of any form of utopia in the sphere of design. "Learning from Las Vegas," then, is a program. It is the program of counter-utopia, against the "all or nothing" of the great ideal models. Undeniably, those visionary exercises in designing the future of the city—the *villes radieuses* of the old and new sort—have now lost the propulsive force they once had. In fact, the proposals are no longer even credible, because experience has shown that they can no longer be realized—at least not without degrading, banalizing, weakening, and even massacring their original intention.[1] So far as that is concerned, the apologists for Las Vegas are right. But they are not right in the fundamental conclusion they draw, when they maintain that known, tangible, and realizable vileness is preferable to unknown, hypothetical, and unrealizable excellence.

The alternative to the abstract utopia of ideal models cannot be possibilistic capitulation; rather, it must consist in the overcoming of that false alternative by means of a "general theory of design praxis."[2] Such an organic complex of criteria directed toward innovative action should help us to generate

67

a fruitful relationship between "critical consciousness" and "design consciousness" within the specific context of recent capitalist society. Or, to put it another way: it will help generate a fruitful relationship between, on the one hand, the exigencies of the "critical consciousness," which cannot stop being critical without ceasing to be consciousness; and, on the other hand, the exigencies of "design consciousness," which cannot abdicate its will to perform without ceasing to be design: between the positive negativeness of criticism and the negative positiveness of design.

The program implicit in this new theory calls to mind Ernst Bloch's "concrete utopia." The connection is not unjustified, for a link in fact exists between the two. But the connection must be understood not in terms of continuity, but rather of dialectic contraposition. The new theory proposes nothing less than a fundamental reversal in the relationship that exists in Bloch's model between the utopian component and the concrete component, to the extent that it tends to minimize the utopian component, which is speculative, and to maximize the concrete, which is technical.

To better understand the program of the new theory, we must now stop and analyze, even if only briefly, why the "concrete utopia" is considered both too utopian and not concrete enough. Although Bloch's theory is more explicit than others that have tried to link utopia and reality,[3] it has obviously not proved to be very malleable when transferred to the realm of contingent reality. That is particularly paradoxical in a theory of anticipation which is unique in defining itself as the "praxis of concrete utopia,"[4] that is to say, a theory that wants to play a guiding role in the factual flux of history.

With the guidance of Marx, Bloch has established that critical consciousness is the basic moving force in any future-oriented praxis, and that surely must be considered enormous progress. But the discussion cannot stop there. Another step

68

forward, which Bloch hesitated to take, would consist in recognizing that if critical consciousness wants to operate efficiently in the realm of action, it must also be the critical consciousness of technical processuality.

In our civilization, in fact, we cannot recognize a praxis that does not explain itself in terms of technical processuality, and that has only categorical, not empirical reference. In *Das Prinzip Hoffnung*, Bloch tries persistently to find a conceptual area impervious to the constricting infiltration both of utopianism and of traditional empiricism. "To attach oneself to things and to avoid them: both are wrong attitudes,"[5] he says. Still, despite his well-known speculative prolixity, Bloch fails in his repeated attempts to furnish us with an operable version of his theory. He manages to avoid falling back into traditional utopianism to the extent that he defines "concrete utopia" principally as "a critical analysis of the present";[6] but his polemical hostility against any form of empiricism leads him to neglect the objective links necessary in any form of anticipation that seeks to become reality.[7]

In recent times, the idea that "concrete utopia" is a sort of utopia-intervention, that is to say, a "utopia in action," has gained a great deal of currency. In our opinion, that is an interpretation without foundation. Bloch's utopia in fact lacks all the prerequisites for a role of that kind. "Concrete utopia" rejects with contemptuous hostility all close contact with the world of contingency, so as to avoid any eventual influence of empiricism, which it does not distinguish from opportunism. Utopia in action, on the contrary, can only realize itself inasmuch as it is capable of breaking through mightily into the world of contingency; within the framework of empiricism (but not of opportunism), it must advance its specific innovative and even revolutionary mission. Furthermore, "concrete utopia" entrusts the task of verifying the factual plausibility of its hypotheses *a posteriori* to a future instance—to a generic

69

sort of socialism; but utopia in action prefers to assume this task itself, *a priori* (or at least during the unfolding of its action).

Since we do not accept the identification of "concrete utopia" with utopia in action, it is important now to emphasize that it is because we have substantial doubts about its concreteness. It should be evident by now that the concreteness of a utopia is tested in the context of action. But to be more precise, we should say: in the context of *effective* action. And that brings us to the problem of technical processuality mentioned earlier. In the final analysis, "concrete utopia" lost its concreteness because it failed to make its arguments technical—that is, it failed to indicate what instrumental means (actions, procedures or stratagems) it would need to overcome the obstinate viscosity of history.

We have spoken of the urgent necessity for a "general theory of design praxis" to overcome the categorical and above all the operative precariousness of "concrete utopia." Unfortunately, and contrary to our earlier belief, we must admit at this point that the process of conceptualizing such a theory cannot be brought to a happy conclusion only by means of a critical examination of Bloch's "utopia." At this moment, it is perhaps more important to look into a new version of "concrete utopia," which also claims to be the dialectical opposite of the preceding version. We refer to the "concrete utopia" which some currents of youthful dissent are celebrating today as the great attempt at "concretization" of "concrete utopia," using that or some other name for it.

In appearance, the new version is antagonistic to the earlier one. The traditional "concrete utopia," as we have just seen, cannot give credible assurance that it is a utopia in action; but the new version claims to be that and only that. If the first believes in the role of design—that is to say, if it prefers, in Bloch's words, to see "the world as a concrete field of design"

(*Welt als konkretes Entwurfsfeld*), the second factiously denies the role of design.[8]

Still, such differences lose much of their dramatic quality and their content when we discover that the two versions agree on a fundamental point. They have in common a profound aversion to any form of applied rationality, and to any technical assessment of the plausibility of their hypotheses. Analyzing Bloch's "concrete utopia," we already arrived at the conclusion that without a technical assessment, the concreteness of utopian argument is a fiction. The same is true for the so-called utopia in action, though here the consequence that follows is in a way even more grave. For a speculative construct like Bloch's "concrete utopia," the loss of concreteness is an exclusively philosophical calamity; but for a utopia in action, it is a calamity that compromises its very reason for being.

It is indeed absurd for a utopia that proclaims action to be reduced to silence precisely in the field of action. And yet, that is what happens. Technical silence puts concreteness to flight, and immediately establishes the silence of action. And all this with the furtive help of logical silence.[9] Therefore, the best way to determine whether a utopia in action deserves that name, the best way to know whether we are faced with a reality or with a mere verbal fancy, is to submit it to the test of concreteness, that is to say, to a verification of the degree of technical and logical consistency of its operative proposals, be they long or short term.

There are to be sure a few utopias in action that can stand the test successfully. But that is not true for the sort of utopias in action we have been discussing here. Their verification generally results in the humiliating denial of any "concreteness" whatever.

At this point, it might be useful to give an example. In 1968 the German review *Kursbuch* published a discussion be-

71

tween its editor, Hans M. Enzensberger, and Rudi Dutschke, Bernd Rabehl, and Christian Semler, on the subject "Is there a revolutionary future for the highly industrialized nations?"[10] Toward the end, Enzensberger tries to force his interlocutors to be more concrete, and challenges them to propose specific solutions to the problems of the future of Berlin. Their answers are painfully disappointing. They either propose obtuse and banal "common-sense" solutions in no way different from those of the most traditional reform movements; or, on the contrary, they venture hypotheses of such speculative temerity that is impossible to determine on what concrete facts they might be based.

We are not questioning the intellectual, personal, or political integrity of these men. What we are trying to emphasize is the instrumental and therefore operative weakness of the model of behavior that orients their action.[11] In other words, we are questioning the kind of utopia in action that exhausts all its reserves in agitation, and then presents itself stuttering, inept, and inexpert before contingent problems.

We must recognize that such utopia in action, because of the rational anemia with which it faces the test of concreteness, is doomed to failure from the start. In other words, already at the point of departure, the paradise it promises is a paradise lost.

We saw earlier that rationality in its most spurious form, as "bourgeois coldness," is accused not wrongly of having been and still being in the service of repressive power. But that does not warrant the hasty deduction, made by some theoreticians of worldwide dissent, that the abandonment of every form of rationality is the only way to save us from the possibility of new violence from "bourgeois coldness."

To do that, we are convinced, would lead to the exact opposite of the desired goal. For it is obvious that the abandonment of every other form of rationality would assure "bourgeois coldness" an ever-greater freedom of action in the exercise of its spurious rationality.

In the final analysis, utopia in action is possible only if we rebuild, on new foundations, our faith in the revolutionary function of applied rationality. That is the only context in which the notion of a "design praxis" can make any sense. And we are quite aware that to do so might reopen the debate concerning the relationship between design and revolution, in all its ramifications.

In the course of this essay we have indicated often how wrong it is to believe that design is revolution and that design is an alternative to revolution—two hypotheses which, from a certain point of view, can signify the same thing. But we certainly did not mean to have the argument considered closed. On the contrary, our intention was to show its complexity, and thereby to forestall the self-satisfaction implicit in certain very gross simplifications.

One thing, at least, can be definitely established: the debate on the relationship between design and revolution cannot be used as an alibi to keep putting off the application, on a massive scale, of environmental design and planning, on which our destiny may well depend. As we believe we have shown, the deterioration of our environment has reached such a degree that any further postponement, however brief, may end by substantially compromising our survival. We must therefore begin now, even if the relationships between design and revolution are not yet definitively defined.

Although this appeal for an immediate commitment is fully justified under the present circumstances, we are not unaware of the conceptual precariousness behind it. The first objection that can and surely will be made is that ours is an attitude of conciliation. In other words, because of a pressing environmental situation, we are hastily backing a new sort of ideology of mediation. The criticism is pertinent, for it denounces a rather vulnerable aspect of our argument, namely, the claim that designing can have a relative innovative autonomy when faced with the agents principally responsible for environmental attrition. The problem is certainly not new. In the last twenty-five years it has been the philosophical obstacle encountered by everyone who has tried to change the world without changing his profession. When a designer—for example, an architect—is persuaded that he can contribute *as a designer* to the transformation of society, he can act in that direction only to the extent in which he believes in a relative innovative autonomy of his work. As we have seen, it is mistaken to think that planning is an alternative to revolution, but it is equally mistaken to deny any kind of autonomy to planning. We can still find men today, late epigones of *Vulgärmarxismus* of unhappy memory, who still reject as too conciliatory those intellectuals who, *precisely because they are intellectuals*, try to play a "civil and progressive role."[12] They would like to resolve the problem in the simplest manner: by denying its legitimacy. But that is a way of not solving it, for the problem continues to exist despite everything.

However things are, the designer must act, he must definitely abandon the "waiting room" in which he has been forced to remain until now. And he must act even if he does not know whether in the end autonomy will not prove to be an illusion. His task will be arduous, even unpleasant; but that is no surprise. Elio Vittorini once remarked, almost without bitterness: "The intellectual [*uomo di cultura*] is put to a hard test in every environment."[13] We might add: especially if his sense of responsibility requires him to put every environment to the test, as is the case with the designer.

POSTSCRIPT

THE SCANDAL OF SOCIETY is now culminating in the scandal of nature. The picture is thus complete. Now one can finally say, with good reason, that society and nature belong to the same order of problems. There are not as was once believed two accounts, one with society, and the other with nature. It is now clear that if the account with society does not add up, the one with nature will not add up either. But the contrary is also true, if nature is in crisis and shows all the symptoms of a precocious senility, society will be fatally emptied of any drive toward the future. No one cares about a future so devoid of future. For no one can escape the fact that if nature is so contaminated as to be unable to guarantee human life on this planet, society itself will have no point. But this sort of interpretation, though close to reality, ends by shutting off any possibility of action against the scandal of nature. At bottom, it favors a passive resignation. The same can be said of the tendency to attribute responsibility for this scandal to the congenital and incurable predatory behavior of man. There is no doubt that much of the current and past violence perpetrated against our physical environment is a consequence, at least in part, of our aggressive-destructive disposition toward nature.[1] Nevertheless, nothing is more erroneous than the desire to absolutize the role of these metahistorical factors. There are also historical factors, the conditioning and determining links of our society. The ferocious sack of nature carried out in the last two centuries would be incomprehensible without a careful examination of the operative modalities of these historical factors. In practice that means that the question concerning the scandal of society must precede the question concerning the scandal of nature.[2]

Has the mobilization of the public on the problems of pollution followed this track? Absolutely not. Inasmuch as it is a mobilization that comes "from above," it was intended to stop the problem of pollution from becoming the problem of society. To achieve this aim, it has made use—with success, up to now—of a particularly perfidious expedient, the transformation of a crucial subject like the degradation of the environment into a fashionable—i.e., transitory—theme. And thus was born the fashion of ecology.[3] The mechanics of fashions, of all fashions, are well known. You take a theme, celebrate it for a few months, and then quickly drop it, make it a fossil. In other words, it is declared "out of fashion." Volatilization through diffusion; debilitation through dispersion. The best way to remove a subject from public attention (or at least from public interest) is to force everyone to be concerned with it continually. The ecological fashion offers us a very clear example of that technique. It was brought to the highest degree of propagandistic effervescence; it is now beginning to evaporate; and paradoxically, the noise of the printing presses in its service is rendering it inaudible. Very soon, it will have completed its life cycle. An outward situation that caused lacerating thoughts in us will have become definitely interiorized. It will be spoken of no more. It will no longer "exist." But only on the alienating plane of sublimation, not on the plane of reality.

76

The fact that the ecological fashion is already in full eclipse does not mean that the degradation of our biosphere has already been arrested or is about to be.[4] The problems remain open, perhaps even more open than they were before the ecological fashion. But it must be admitted that it has at least had one positive aspect: It formed an ecological conscience. For the moment, it is still an inconsistent conscience, without roots, easily eradicable. But we can imagine that once the fashion passes, it will be possible to take up once again the efforts that will lead to an essentially critical ecological conscience—critical toward the scandal of society.

NOTES

1. The notion of a "human environment" must be defined at the outset. The most traditional, but at the same time the most correct procedure, is to define the human environment in relation to the animal environment. Whereas animals have only one environment, men have an "artifact-environment." Arnold Gehlen expressed this same view with other words. Animals, he says, have an *Umwelt* (a surrounding world), but they do not have a *Welt* (world). See Arnold Gehlen, *Der Mensch* (Bonn: Athenaeum Verlag, 1955), p. 188. According to Gehlen, the *Welt* of men is distinguished from the *Umwelt* of animals by its instrumental nature. The human *Welt* is an "artifact-environment." At bottom, this is the same as the old idea expressed back in 1934 by the biologist Jacob von Uexküll in his book *Streifzüge durch die Umwelten von Tieren und Menschen: Bedeutungslehre* (Hamburg: Rowohlt, 1956), p. 21. According to him, our environment is a system of artifacts: on the one hand there are operational artifacts (*Werkzeuge*), and on the other there are artifacts for perception (*Merkzeuge*). In other words, the *Welt*, culture in the anthropological sense, is a web of artifact-utensils and artifact-symbols that mutually condition and depend upon each other. See L. A. White, *The Science of Culture* (New York: Grove Press, 1949). "It was the introduction of symbols," says White,

"word-formed symbols, into the tool process that transformed anthropoid tool-behavior into human tool-behavior" (p. 45). On this point, see the chapter *Per uno schema omologico della produzione* in the book by Ferruccio Rossi-Landi, *Il linguaggio come lavoro e come mercato* (Milan: Bompiani, 1968), pp. 141*ff*. On the notion of *Umwelt* in the works of Husserl, see Enzo Paci and Pier Aldo Rovatti, *Persona, mondo circondante, motivazione*, as well as Salvatore Veca, *Implicazioni filosofiche della nozione di ambiente*. Both articles were published in *Aut-Aut* (May and July, 1968), pp. 105–6, 142–71, and 172–82.

2. But this statement does not necessarily mean that the idea of environment never existed before. Though it wore different colors and bore a different name, the idea of environment appeared often (in an embryonic state, to be sure) in the reflections of philosophers of all periods, and particularly in their reflections on the idea of nature. See the study by Robert Lenoble, *Histoire de l'idée de nature* (Paris: Michel, 1969). There it emerges clearly that philosophers from the pre-Socratics to the eighteenth-century rationalists continually dwelled on this theme. They had intuited the limits of the idea of nature and had attempted to go beyond them, trying to bridge the abyss between the reality of nature and the reality of history, between nature and society, and between nature and "human nature." Though it is not permissible to define the idea of environment solely in terms of nature, which human praxis has rendered historically human, there can be no doubt that the modern idea of environment was born and developed in that conceptual context. See also Alfred Schmidt, *Der Begriff der Natur in der Lehre von Marx* (Frankfurt am Main: Europäische Verlagsanstalt, 1962).

3. The phrase "resumption of the debate" does not by any means refer to the current widespread use, or rather abuse, of the idea of alienation; rather, it refers exclusively to the recent work of several Marxist experts who are trying to put the discussion of alienation on a more rigorous plane. An example of this effort is the work by the Italian scholar Giuseppe Bedeschi, *Alienazione e feticismo nel pensiero di Marx* (Bari: Laterza, 1968), a work that makes a serious attempt to resume the argument. The same can

be said of two recent articles, one by Victoria L. Rippere, "Schiller and 'Alienation': Towards a *'Nettoyage de la Situation verbale'*—Some Aspects of the Eighteenth Century Background," in *Mosaic*, 2:1 (1968), 90–109. The other is by Daniel Vidal, "Un cas de faux concept: la notion d'aliénation," in *Sociologie du Travail*, 11:1 (January–March, 1969), 61–82. The first article treats very accurately the historical development of the concept of alienation before Hegel, Feuerbach, and Marx; or, more specifically, the use made of the concept by Rousseau, Herder, Schiller, Novalis, and Fichte. The second article depicts the manner in which the subject has been treated in the 1950s and '60s, especially by the American sociologists Daniel Bell, Melvin Seeman, John W. Evans, Arthur G. Neal, and Dwight D. Dean; and also by such Italian and French sociologists as Giuseppe Bonazzi and Alain Touraine. But obviously, a reconstruction of the historical development of the concept before Hegel, Feuerbach, and Marx, and a treatment of the current state of the subject in the light of the most recent orientations in sociology, are not enough to satisfy the need for a drastic *nettoyage de la situation*, as Rippere called it. The concept of alienation was already ambiguous in Hegel, and no less so in Marx. The pages Hegel dedicated to an analysis of the *sich entfremdete Geist* are perhaps among the most explicit and articulated in his entire philosophical work; but they are also the pages that started the most difficult problems for post-Hegelian thought. See G. W. F. Hegel, *Phänomenologie des Geistes*, in *Sämtliche Werke* (Stuttgart: Fromann Verlag, 1964), II, pp. 372ff. Marx's attempt to turn Hegel's argument inside out (*umstülpen*) without changing its terms has had surprising results. On the one hand the concreteness of the idea of alienation has become ever stronger; on the other hand this very concreteness has made even more evident the conceptual ambiguity (and even oscillation) that was already present in Hegel. See Karl Marx, *Zur Judenfrage* (1843), in *Frühe Schriften* (Cotta Verlag, Stuttgart, 1962), I, eds. H. J. Lieber and P. Furth, pp. 451ff. In the same *Frühe Schriften*, see also *Zur Kritik der Nationalökonomie—ökonomisch-philosophische Manuskripte* (1844), pp. 559ff. At times, Marx identifies *Arbeit* (work) with *Äusserung* (expression, externalization), with *Selbsterzeugung* (self-realization), with *Vergegen-ständlichung* (objectification); but on other occasions, he identifies it with *Entäusserung* (alienation), with *Entfremdung* (estrangement), or with *Verdinglichung* (reification). When Marx speaks of *Arbeit* (work) as an anthropologist or an ontologist, he *almost always* speaks of it in positive terms; but when he speaks as an economist or a revolutionary, he *always* speaks of work in negative terms. This ambiguity of ideas has not yet been overcome by any of the important Marxist experts. Herbert Marcuse was the first to study the subject with an eye to Marx's early works. See his famous essay "Neue Quellen zur Grundlegung des historischen Materialismus" in *Die Gesellschaft, Internationale Revue für Sozialismum und Politik* 9:2 (1932). In that article, Marcuse gives an acute analysis of the subtle implications in Marx's concept of alienation, based on the various ways in which Marx used the term. For example, the difference between *Verdinglichung* ("the positiveness of human reality") and *Vergegenstandlichung* ("the negativeness of human reality"). Marcuse took the theme up again later (1941) in his book *Reason and Revolution: Hegel and the Rise of Social Theory* (Boston: Beacon Press, 1960). Another important contribution was made by G. Della Volpe, *Per la teoria di un umanesimo positivo* (Bologna: Zuffi, 1949). The most complete study of alienation is still H. Popitz, *Der entfremdete Mensch, Zeitkritik und Geschichtsphilosophie des jungen Marx* (Berlin: Aufbau Verlag, 1954), pp. 680ff. In all these publications we can discern an extreme difficulty in arriving at a unified version of the concept of alienation. H. Lefebvre has tried to show that a theory of alienation does not yet exist, and that it can only be developed if we take the dialectical ambiguity implicit in Marx's approach as the point of departure. In his book *Critique de la vie quotidienne —Fondements d'une sociologie de la quotidienneté* (Paris: L' Arche Editeur, 1961), Lefebvre describes the process of *aliénation-desaliénation-nouvelle aliénation*—i.e., the dialectical cycle of the process of alienation. "It is hard," Lefebvre rightly observes, "to find a simple, objective, and general criterion for alienation. Such variety also shows that it is both possible and indispensable to elaborate a typology of alienation" (p. 216). In other words,

Lefebvre considers the variety of the phenomenon a fundamental methodological advantage. His pluralistic approach allows him to identify successfully the various types of alienation; but these various types do not exist in isolation. Each of them, whatever its cause, participates actively in the same dialectical cycle mentioned earlier. But according to Lefebvre, the most dynamogenetic factor of the cycle must be sought in the intersubjective relationship. This is the factor that blocks and unblocks, accelerates or slows down the internal flux of the cycle. This rather unorthodox point of view is proving to be particularly fruitful today, and much more consistent with Marx's thought than it might seem. Obviously, to say that Marx's interpretation of alienation is not contradictory and monolithic is to distort Marx. To be sure, the idea that the source of alienation resides in the system of property is to be found in *Zur Kritik der Nationalökonomie*; but even in that work, we find certain nuances that have not been given sufficient consideration. Nor should we forget the radical "theory of emancipation" clearly formulated by Marx in *Zur Judenfrage*, in which work we find an indirect repudiation of the thesis that the end of private ownership of the means of production—that is to say, the end of the capitalist system—will also mean the automatic liberation of man from every form of alienation. In that fundamental text, Marx writes: "We find that Bauer's error consists in subjecting to criticism *only* the 'Christian state,' and not the state in and of itself; he fails to investigate the *relationship of political emancipation to human emancipation,* and therefore establishes conditions which only an acritical confusion of political emancipation with general human emancipation can justify. . . ." (p. 456). "The limits of political emancipation are immediately evident when we consider that the *state* can free itself of a restriction without making men really free; the state can be a *free state* without men being *free men*" (p. 458). To synthesize, we may say that human emancipation is not dependent upon liberation from any particular form of state, but rather upon liberation from any form of state imaginable. On the subject of the "new alienation" (*neue Entfremdung*) in socialist society, see Ernst Fischer, *Kunst und Koexistenz* (Reinbeck bei Hamburg: Rowohlt Verlag, 1966), p.

103; and, also by Fischer, *Auf den Spuren der Wirklichkeit* (Reinbeck bei Hamburg: Rowohlt Verlag, 1968), pp. 194*ff.* In the context of this note, we must not fail to mention the Marxists of the current that is rightly or wrongly called "structuralist." According to these scholars, alienation is a problem of no scientific interest, a pseudoproblem, one of the many pre-Marxian ideological residues to be found in Marx, or rather in the "young Marx." And yet, paradoxically enough, it was precisely one of the most famous representatives of that current, Louis Althusser, who unwittingly opened a new prospect in the debate on alienation. Reading Marx with his bizarre *symptômale* method, Althusser developed a temerarious but fruitful interpretation of the epistemology contained in the early work *Zur Kritik der Nationalökonomie.* He reopened the question of the relationship between consciousness and reality, attributing to the products of consciousness (including its "alienated" products) their own specific concreteness. See Louis Althusser, Jacques Rancière, and Pierre Macherey, *Reading Capital,* trans. by Étienne Balibar (New York: Pantheon, 1971).

4. The paternity of the word "ecology" is attributed to the German zoologist Ernst Haeckel (*Ökologie,* from *oikos,* house). But the first public appearance of the word came later, in 1895, when it was used by the Danish botanist Warming. See G. L. Clarke, *Elements of Ecology* (New York: John Wiley, 1954).

5. The term "human ecology" was introduced by Park and Burgess in 1921. An excellent depiction of this new discipline may be found in the work by G. A. Theodorson, *Studies in Human Ecology* (New York: Harper & Row, 1961). The study of the psychological aspects of "human ecology" has developed recently as "ecological psychology." Generally speaking, it continues the scientific tradition that began with Kurt Lewin, Egon Brunswick, and Fritz Heider. Some recent studies that might be consulted with profit are E. P. Willems, "An Ecological Orientation in Psychology," *Merrill-Palmer Quarterly of Behavior and Development* 11:4 (October, 1965), 317–43; S. B. Sells, "Ecology and the Science of Psychology," *Multivariate Behavioural Research,* 1:2 (April, 1966), 131–44; R. G. Barker, "Exploration in Ecological Psychology," *American Psychologist* (January, 1965), 1–14.

6. The American biotechnicians L. J. Fogel, A. J. Owens, and M. J. Walsh, in their book *Artificial Intelligence Through Simulated Evolution* (New York: John Wiley, 1966), maintain the thesis that the appearance of human consciousness was originally merely an "artifact of the natural experiment called evolution." In other words, it was merely an emergency procedure taken by nature in a state of emergency. Consciousness was merely a new factor, whose precise function was to help recuperate the equilibrium of the ecological universe which, for reasons we can scarcely intuit, seemed definitely condemned to universal catastrophe. Nor is that all. According to the interpretation of these biotechnicians, man long ago fulfilled the role assigned to him by "Evolution," so that today he no longer represents a factor for order, but for disorder. Following this line, they hypothesize that the only escape from such a situation lies in the creation by nature of a new creature (an artificial intelligence, for example) that could replace man, and be more adaptable to an ecological universe with other needs. Though it is interesting, this theory really signifies a return to the finalistic personalization of nature, very typical of a neovitalism of obvious metaphysical inspiration. See also L. J. Fogel, *Biotechnology—Concepts and Applications* (Englewood Cliffs, N.J.: Prentice-Hall, 1963), particularly the chapter "Human Decision-Making," pp. 324ff. It is very curious to see how these modern supporters of *L'Homme Machine* of the great La Mettrie (see Aram Vartanian, *La Mettrie's L'Homme Machine* (Princeton: Princeton University Press, 1960), dogmatic representatives of modern biological neomechanism, are capable of the most unusual conceptual acrobatics: they can, for instance, use in defense of their theories almost the same arguments used by Hans Driesch and Henri Bergson, and exactly the same arguments used by Pierre Teilhard de Chardin in *The Future of Man* (New York: Harper & Row, 1964). "We may have supposed," Teilhard writes, "that the human species, being matured, has reached the limit of its development. Now we see that it is still in an *embryonic state*. Science can discern, in the hundreds of thousands (probably millions) of years lying ahead of the Mankind we know, a deep if

still obscure fringe of the 'ultra-human'" (pages 294–5). In contrast to the concept of Teilhard de Chardin, compare the polemical position taken by the English biologist P. B. Medawar in *The Art of the Soluble* (London: Methuen, 1967), p. 73.

7. One of the first to perceive the value of literary observation to scientific research was Sigmund Freud. In 1910, in his essay "Beiträge zur Psychologie des Liebeslebens," in *Gesammelte Werke* (Frankfurt am Main: S. Fischer Verlag, 1964), 4th ed., VIII, Freud wrote: "Poets also have command over many qualities that allow them to solve such a problem. Above all they possess a fine sensibility for perceiving the secret movements in the psyche of another person, and the courage to let their own unconscious express itself" (p. 66). On the specific contribution made by Dostoevsky, see Kurt Lewin, *Principles of Topological Psychology* (New York: McGraw-Hill, 1963), p. 63. For Proust's contribution, see Fritz Heider, "The Description of the Psychological Environment in the Work of Marcel Proust," *Psychological Issues*, 1:3 (1959), 85–107 [originally published in *Character and Personality*, 9 (1941), 295–314]. "Novelists who have the reputation of being good psychologists," Heider observes, "can give evidence of their knowledge of human nature in different ways. . . . in Proust's work we find many points of contact with academic psychology" (p. 85). For further clarification of the importance of "common-sense psychology," see also Fritz Heider, *The Psychology of Interpersonal Relations* (London: John Wiley, 1958), pp. 5ff.

8. There are some very valuable contributions to the study of the film, particularly from the point of view of macrosociology (Siegfried Kracauer, Paul Lazarsfeld, T. W. Adorno, Léo Handel), of the psychology of aesthetic perception (Rudolf Arnheim), of iconographic revelation (Erwin Panofsky), of the *philosophie du cinéma* (Gilbert Cohen-Seat), of Marxist epistemology (Galvano Della Volpe), and of semiotic aesthetics (Christian Metz, Gillo Dorfles, Roland Barthes, Umberto Eco, Jean Mitry, Gianfranco Bettetini). But we lack an "environmental microsociology of the cinema"—that is to say, a serious study of the contribution made by the film world to the determination of the

behavior of men toward other men and toward their microenvironment.

CHAPTER TWO

1. "Americans," writes the American designer R. S. Latham, "are apparently unaware of such a simple, out-of-balance relationship as the following: a 120-pound woman will get into, start, and drive a 3000-pound vehicle five city blocks, spend the time to find a parking space, walk through a supermarket, return, drive back, and re-enter her home, in order to carry one small sack of oranges a distance she could have walked in half the time." "The Artifact as a Cultural Cipher," in *Who Designs America?* ed. L. B. Holland (Garden City, N.Y.: Doubleday, 1966), p. 259.

2. See Theodosius Dobzhansky, *Mankind Evolving* (New Haven: Yale University Press, 1962), p. 89. "Man," says Dobzhansky, "is a part of his own environment: he influences his environment, as well as being influenced by it." This concept was recently taken up from a very original perspective and developed by Serge Moskovici, *Essai sur l'histoire humaine de la nature* (Paris: Flammarion, 1968).

3. The analysis of Lewis S. Feuer, in "The Masochist Mode in Asian Civilization" in *The Scientific Intellectual* (New York: Basic Books, 1963), pp. 340ff., does not affect this judgment. His views, which are based fundamentally on the opinions of Joseph Needham, *Science and Civilization in China* (Cambridge, Eng.: Cambridge University Press, 1954) are valid only for a certain period in the history of China and Japan. Moreover, J. M. Bocheński demonstrated in his introduction to Hindu logic that if there are indeed important differences between the structure of Greek and Hindu logic, there are also very substantial similarities. See *Formale Logik* (Freiburg and Munich: Verlag K. Alber, 1956), pp. 481ff. There is the danger of false generalization in preconceptions concerning Western culture. There is, for example, the very widespread notion that the idea of progress was absolutely foreign to "classical antiquity." The work that best represents that notion is J. B. Bury, *The Idea of Progress* (New York: Dover

Publications, 1955). Ludwig Edelstein, in his book *The Idea of Progress in Classical Antiquity* (Baltimore: Johns Hopkins Press, 1967), proved that Bury's approach was lacking in foundation. See Rodolfo Mondolfo, *El infinito en el pensamiento de la antigüedad clásica* (Buenos Aires: Imán, 1952). In this work the author does away with a similar and also very deeply rooted preconception, namely that Greek culture was incapable of conceiving the infinite.

4. G. B. Vico, *Dell'antichissima sapienze italica*, in *Opere* (Milan and Naples: R. Ricciardi, 1953), p. 292.

5. Ernst Bloch, *Das Prinzip Hoffnung* (Frankfurt am Main: Suhrkamp Verlag, 1959).

6. Samuel Butler, *Erewhon and Erewhon Revisited* (London: Everyman Library, 1965). First published in 1872.

7. Arno Schmidt, *Die Gelehrtenrepublik* (Karlsruhe: Stahlberg Verlag, 1957).

8. There is no doubt that the will to plan is subtly linked to the reality of desire. See Vittorio Gregotti, *Il territorio dell'architettura* (Milan: Feltrinelli, 1966): "I do not believe one can speak of a plan," writes Gregotti, "without speaking of desire. Design is the mode by which we try to put into action the satisfaction of one of our desires" (p. 11). With that, Gregotti places design very close to that which, for many years now, has been the central theme of Surrealist ethics and aesthetics: desire as the original moving force behind every action that tends to change life; desire as an act of designing which will sooner or later bring about innovation. In other words, the Surrealists consider desire to be something always potentially revolutionary. "Man," says André Breton, "proposes and disposes. It is up to him alone to keep complete control of himself, that is to say, to keep those of his desires that become ever more dangerous in an anarchical state" —*Les Manifestes du Surréalisme* (Paris: Editions du Sagittaire, 1946), p. 34. But even the very fact of "keeping desires in an anarchical state" is a matter of designing, for it implies the desire for an order capable of guaranteeing the permanent expansion of desires. This hypothetical order is always in conflict with the pre-established order. Here is Paul Eluard's answer to the famous

Enquête sur le désir: "The most noble of desires is the desire to fight all the obstacles that bourgeois society puts before the realization of man's vital desires, be they those of his body or those of his imagination"—*Livre d'identité*, ed. R. D. Valette (Vevey: C. Tchou, 1967), p. 44. We can trace the precursors of this philosophy of subversive desire, as well as the precursors of *amour fou* in the service of revolution, to those great heretics of romanticism and symbolism in the nineteenth century: Petrus Borel, Nerval, Baudelaire, Lautréamont, and Rimbaud. After a long period of stoical repression, these men had the courage to exalt desire for the first time. Epictetus, the philosopher and slave, had written: "As for desire, suppress it, for now"—*Enchiridion* (Indianapolis: Bobbs-Merrill). That "for now" has always perplexed scholars. As a matter of fact, no one knows why Epictetus wanted to make this renunciation of desire provisional. Perhaps he too had conceived of a probable world without repression, a world in which one could speak of desire without speaking of design.

9. C. Wright Mills, *Power, Politics, and People* (New York: Ballantine Books, 1962). Originally the article "Man in the Middle: The Designer" was published in the review *Industrial Design* (November, 1958).

CHAPTER THREE

1. See G. C. Argan, "Strutture ambientali" in *Edilizia*, 14:17 (September 21, 1968). In this introductory report to the 17th Convention of Rimini, Argan defends the thesis of an irreversible crisis in the design of industrial objects. He writes: "The design of objects for industrial production is no longer of any interest to us; that stage is past, the battle lost. Our analysis must start with the crisis in Design, with the failure of the Bauhaus program" (p. 4). Bruno Zevi expresses a similar attitude. In his recent article "L'orco conformista ha mangiato l'architetto" in *L'Espresso* 14:28 (July 14, 1968), Zevi in fact speaks of "the exhaustion of a discipline that had deteriorated to a trade: design" (p. 20). It is difficult to understand the meaning of such assertions. Undoubtedly the word design is being used here in a very particular

sense. Strictly speaking, industrial civilization without the application of design to its objects, that is to say, without planning or design, is unthinkable. But for Argan and Zevi, that seems not to be the case. For them, the design of objects for industrial production is merely a minor modality: it is a mere trade, a form of action which in the long run cannot survive. It seems very evident that their interpretation contains traces of Crocian aesthetics, according to which anything that does not result from the will to expression is not to be recognized as art, or as a valid cultural phenomenon. On the relationship between design and art, see our essays "Design-Objekte und Kunst-Objekte" in *Ulm*, 7 (January, 1963), 18–22; and "Ist Produktgestaltung eine Künstlerische Tätigkeit?" *loc. cit.*, 10–11 (May, 1964), 74–76. See also Dino Formaggio, *L'idea di artisticità* (Milan: Editrice Ceschina, 1962), pp. 237ff.

2. T. W. Adorno, *Negative Dialektik* (Frankfurt am Main: Suhrkamp Verlag, 1966), p. 357. By the same author see also *Prismen—Kulturkritik und Gesellschaft* (Munich: Deutsche Taschenbuch Verlag, 1963), p. 26; and *Eingriffe—neue kritische Modelle* (Frankfurt am Main: Suhrkamp Verlag, 1963), p. 68.

3. Also in *Negative Dialektik*, p. 354. The idea of "bourgeois coldness" as Adorno understands it can be traced back to Schiller. In *Uber die ästhetische Erziehung der Menschen* in *Gesammelte Werke* (Bielefeld: C. Bertelsmann Verlag, 1958), V, p. 388, Schiller writes: "The abstract thinker often has a cold heart, for he dissects impressions, whereas they affect the soul only in their entirety. The businessman often has a narrow heart, because his imagination is locked in the uniform circle of his profession, unable to open itself to other ways of thinking" (1795).

4. The Cartesian theme of looking at the world impassively, with a "dry eye," was taken up again by the bourgeois culture of the Victorian age. It is the same theme implicit in the Pre-Raphaelites' need to "look at the world without eyelids." See R. Runcini, *Illusione e paura nel mondo borghese da Dickens a Orwell* (Bari: Laterza, 1968), p. 27.

5. This concept is opposed to the one maintained by György Lukács in his book *Die Zerstörung der Vernunft* (Berlin: Aufbau

Verlag, 1952). Lukács maintains that there is an absolute linearity in the philosophical process that leads to fascism. In his view, the responsibility lies exclusively with (German) irrationalism, to which he attributes a perfect "unity of development." This development includes Schelling, Schopenhauer, Kierkegaard, Dilthey, Simel, Spengler, Scheler, Heidegger, Jaspers, Max Weber, Mannheim . . . and Rosenberg. The simplicism of Lukács's approach recalls the old book by the American Catholic George Santayana, *Egotism in German Philosophy*. From a very different point of view, to be sure, the book tried to attribute responsibility for the Prussian military adventure of the First World War exclusively to the ideas of Goethe, Kent, Fichte, Nietzsche, and Schopenhauer.

6. Max Horkheimer and T. W. Adorno, *Dialektik der Aufklärung, Philosophische Fragmente* (Amsterdam: Querido Verlag, 1947). The point of view maintained by Horkheimer and Adorno has been very severely criticized by several Marxist scholars. See Lucio Colletti, *Il marxismo e Hegel* (Bari: Laterza, 1969), pp. 332*ff.* See also Galvano Della Volpe, *Critica della ideologia contemporanea* (Rome: Editori Riuniti, 1967), pp. 61*ff.*

7. The speech Churchill gave at Westminster College in Fulton, Missouri, on March 15, 1946, is considered by many historians the "official" beginning of the cold war. "If there is to be a Third World War," writes D. F. Fleming, "Churchill's speech in Missouri will constitute the primary document for an understanding of its origins." *Storia della guerra fredda—1917–1960* (Milan: Feltrinelli, 1964), p. 446. On the same subject see Sergio Segre, "Dalla sconfitta del nazismo alla logica dei blocchi militari" in *Critica marxista*, 4–5 (July-October 1968), 112–38.

8. On the *Déclaration universelle des droits de l'homme*, see the recent UNESCO publication *Le droit d'être un homme* (Paris: Laffont, 1968).

9. Cited by Günther Anders in "Der Amerikanische Krieg in Vietnam oder philosophisches Wörterbuch heute" in *Das Argument*, 45:5–6 (December, 1967), 350.

10. This may be the time to point out that cruelty, as the term is used here, has a very vast signification, but at the same

time a very precise one. In this field, ambiguity, even if unconscious, may lead us to complicity. That is why we cannot accept the paradoxical assertions of Antonin Artaud, despite their undeniable literary value. See "Lettres sur la cruauté" in *Oeuvres complètes* (Paris: Gallimard, 1964). "In this case of cruelty, it is not a matter of sadism or of blood, at least not exclusively. . . . The identification of cruelty with torture is only one aspect of the question. . ." (p. 121). "Effort is cruelty; existence through effort is cruelty" (p. 123). No linguistic acrobatics, no subtlety of analysis can allow us to forget the obstinate concreteness of cruelty. Our definition is simple, perhaps even banal, but certainly not ambiguous. For us, cruelty is an act of violent aggression exercised by one individual, group, or community against another individual, group or community. The aim of cruelty—even of the so-called gratuitous cruelty of the sadist—is to inflict a physical or moral hurt on someone. The difference between physical and moral cruelty is that the former never excludes the latter, whereas the latter may have an effect on the physical integrity of the victim only if it is pushed beyond certain limits. Furthermore, there is a form of cruelty against oneself, which is often a sublimated form of cruelty against others. The most explicit form of cruelty is torture. It is precisely torture that establishes clearly the boundaries between the coercive totalitarian state and the persuasive totalitarian state. In the former, torture is congenial to the system. "Torture: a strange manner of interrogating people," Voltaire observed sarcastically in his *Dictionnaire philosophique*. In the latter kind of state, it is only a sporadic relapse, and is part of a procedure not congenial to the system. The modern totalitarian state is always coercive in the beginning, but sooner or later always becomes persuasive. This is the conviction of Jacques Ellul, *The Technological Society* (New York: Vintage Books, 1967): "These things [torture] did certainly exist; but they represented transient traits, not real characteristics of the totalitarian state. . . . Torture and excess are the acts of persons who use them as a means of releasing a supressed need for power. This does not interest us here. It does not represent the true face of the completely technical totalitarian state. In such a state nothing useless exists; there is no torture; torture is a wasteful expenditure of psychic energy which destroys salvageable resources without producing useful results" (p. 287). If Ellul is right, torture will very probably disappear; but it will certainly be survived by cruelty.

11. Georges Bataille, *L'expérience intérieure* (Paris: Gallimard, 1954), p. 230.

12. Because of their cult of "black humor," the Surrealists have often been accused of being ideological protofascists. We do not share that opinion, for we believe "black humor" contains certain positive aspects, especially as an antidote to "white humor," which is often a form of evasion. At any rate, in some Surrealists we find a kind of "black humor" that cannot escape embarrassing comparisons. Jacques Rigaut, for example, writes: "The surest form of humor still resides in depriving people of their little lives for no particular reason, just to laugh"—*La Révolution Surrealiste*, 12 (December 15, 1929), 55-7.

13. Cited in Leon Poliakov, *Bréviare de la haine—Le IIIe Reich et les Juifs* (Paris: Calmann-Lévy, 1951), p. 14.

14. That is precisely what Ernst Bloch advised Rudi Dutschke in the famous conversation at Bad Boll in West Germany. "Even in the revolutionary movement there must be gaiety; for the most part it has been lacking hitherto." See "Heiterkeit in die Revolution bringen" in *Spiegel*, 10 (1968), 57.

15. Fyodor Dostoevsky, "The Gambler," in *The Short Novels of Dostoevsky* (New York: Dial Press, 1945).

16. But that is not all there is to say on violence. The theme recurs like an obsession and is hard to avoid. The truth is that any rigorous reflection on the social destiny of man is always transformed, sooner or later, into a painful reflection on the role of violence in history. Painful because violence has always been mortifying to rationality. In the final analysis, violence is always violence against reason, in all cases. We might try to call reason to its aid—that is, we might want to say it is right; but violence has a fatally irrational side. Upon the slightest contact with the subject of violence, rationality comes into conflict with itself and becomes, so to speak, unreasonable. And that happens not only

when we try to justify violence rationally, but also when we try to condemn it. In fact, when we want to refute violence rationally, we do it, according to Popper, in the name of an "irrational faith in the attitude of reasonableness." See the chapter "Utopia and Violence" in Karl R. Popper, *Conjectures and Refutations: The Growth of Scientific Knowledge* (New York: Harper Torchbooks, 1963), pp. 355ff. On the relationship between rationality and violence, see also Hannah Arendt, *On Violence* (New York: Harcourt Brace Jovanovich, 1966). Of course, these assertions might seem at first to be fictitious speculative constructions. Rationality and violence are forced to do the most exhausting acrobatics. Nevertheless, such dialectical practices have had an important function, for they have impeded the relationship between rationality and violence from crystallizing into some dogmatic (and definitive) interpretative scheme. The history of modern thought—at least from Sorel to today—shows that clearly. As we will recall, Sorel spoke of "bourgeois strength" and "proletarian violence," identifying the first with authority and the second with revolt. See Georges Sorel, *Reflections on Violence* (New York: Collier-Macmillan, 1961). This definition has become anachronistic: contrary to what was happening at the time Sorel wrote his book, there exist in the world today various examples of proletarian strength (i.e., authority), and not a few examples of bourgeois violence (i.e., revolt). Obviously the traditional categories of Sorel have lost currency. We cannot continue to identify violence with revolt. It would be closer to reality to recognize that violence is always, at least potentially, in the service of established power, whereas action directed against the supremacy of that power cannot be defined as violence *tout court*, but as counterviolence, i.e., as a particular form of violence that expresses itself in terms of a liberating reaction against the coercive action of power. That is why violence and counterviolence cannot be isolated. Between them there exists a conceptual and factual relationship of promiscuous complicity. They act like connected vessels: when the level of one goes up, the level of the other automatically goes up too. This new way of interpreting violence attained its most incisive formulation in Sartre: "Violence always presents itself as *counterviolence*, that is to say, as an answer to

94

the violence of the Other. . . . Whether it is a matter of killing, of torturing, of subjecting, simply of mystifying, my aim is to suppress the liberty of others as I would a hostile force, a force that can chase me away from the field of action and make of me 'one man too many' condemned to death." See Jean Paul Sartre, *Critique de la Raison Dialectique* (Paris: Gallimard, 1960), I, p. 209. The concept of counterviolence plays a fundamental role today in the articulation of the radical revolutionary thought. We find it, for instance, in Fanon, who undoubtedly derived it from Sartre's theory on the relationship between the colonizer and the colonized. Fanon was able to enrich it and even to transform it in the light of his vast and active personal experience as an anticolonialist. See Frantz Fanon, *The Wretched of the Earth* (New York: Grove Press, 1968). He has permeated the theme of violence with partisanship, inasmuch as he has declared that violence is evil, always reactionary, whereas counterviolence is good, always revolutionary. But Manichean partisanship is one of those mortifications of rationality we mentioned earlier. It is the decision that terror is univocal: the terror only of the Other. It is a rejection of the "plurality of terrors" (Sartre). At this point we must admit that the problem is no longer soluble; nor can any discussion of tolerance help us, because everything that can be said of violence is transferable to tolerance. The subject of tolerance also runs aground on the reefs of partisanship. Against the false tolerance of the oppressor arises the true tolerance of the oppressed—that is to say, the countertolerance that can be identified with counterviolence. See Herbert Marcuse, "Repressive Tolerance," in R. P. Wolff, B. Moore Jr., and Herbert Marcuse, *A Critique of Pure Tolerance* (Boston: Beacon Press, 1965). The attempts to neutralize this argument scientifically have certainly shed some light on important aspects of the etiology of violence, but they have not resolved the difficulty we have pointed out in this note. As an example of those attempts, we may cite the recent bio-behavioristic theory of aggression. See Konrad Lorenz, *On Aggression* (New York: Bantam, 1967); and A. M. Becker et al., *Bis hierher und nicht weiter—ist die menschliche Aggression unbefriedbar?* ed. A. Mitscherlich (Munich: Piper Verlag, 1969).

CHAPTER FOUR

1. Robert Boguslaw, *The New Utopians: A Study of System Design and Social Change* (Englewood Cliffs, N.J.: Prentice-Hall, 1965).

2. *Ibid.*, pp. 1*ff.*

3. This key concept of technocratic ideology was first enunciated in 1824, in the *Système de politique positive*, the third part of Saint-Simon's *Catéchisme des Industriels*, written at his commission by Auguste Comte. *Oeuvres de Claude-Henri de Saint-Simon* (Paris: Editions Anthropos, 1966), IV, *réimpression anastatique de l'édition de 1875*. "Scientific politics excludes anything that is arbitrary, for such politics eradicates the absolute and the vague, which were the origins and support of arbitrariness. . . . The arbitrary, then, must necessarily come to an end. The government of things will replace the government of men: then there will truly be *law* in politics, in the real and philosophical sense given to that expression by the illustrious Montesquieu" (p. 331). But the true paternity of this idea must be attributed to Saint-Simon himself. In his work *L'Organisateur* (1819–20) we read: "It cannot be repeated often enough that the only useful action man can take is the action of man on things. The action of man on man is always, per se, harmful to the species, because of the double destruction of forces it brings about" (p. 192).

4. We are speaking here in very general terms of models as replicas; but it should be remembered that in the modern "theory of models," the replica is only *one* of the many functions of the model, and not the only one. K. M. Sayre, for example, has established three different forms of "model": (*a*) replica; (*b*) formalization; and (*c*) simulation. See K. M. Sayre, *Recognition: A Study in the Philosophy of Artificial Intelligence* (Notre Dame, Ind.: University of Notre Dame Press, 1965), p. 4. See also the book edited by K. M. Sayre and F. J. Crosson, *The Modeling of Mind, Computers and Intelligence* (Notre Dame, Ind.: University of Notre Dame Press, 1965), p. 5. Other classifications of models also exist, such as those of Max Black, *Models and Metaphors, Studies in Language and Philosophy* (Ithaca, N.Y.: Cornell

University Press, 1966), pp. 222*ff*.: (*a*) scale models; (*b*) analogue models; and (*c*) mathematical models. Or this other classification devised by Anatol Rapoport, following the lead of Karl Deutsch: (*a*) heuristic models; (*b*) forecasting models; and (*c*) measurement models. See Anatol Rapoport, *Operational Philosophy* (New York: Harper & Row, 1953), p. 207.

5. See Anatol Rapoport, *Two Persons Game Theory—The Essential Ideas* (Ann Arbor: University of Michigan Press, 1966). "To be sure, the geometer deals not with 'circular objects,' but with circles. That is to say, the conceptual act of abstracting circularity from all circular objects was performed long enough ago to have been institutionalized in our language and in our science. . . . The game theoretician is in a more difficult position. The aspects of decisions in conflict situations which he considers to be essential are not immediately evident to the mind as is the circularity of circular objects. . . . We are more emotionally involved with conflicts than with shapes of objects" (pp. 5*ff*). See also, by the same author, *Fights, Games, and Debates* (Ann Arbor: University of Michigan Press, 1960).

6. We know full well that aside from McNamara, there are other personalities who have had considerable influence on the official (or quasi-official) "diplo-military" doctrine of the United States. One of them is Herman Kahn, Director of the Hudson Institute, whose views on the subject have caused bitter and clamorous debate over the past few years. Never before was the theory of the "equilibrium of terror" presented more explicitly (or better, more cynically) than it was in his book *On Thermonuclear War* (Princeton: Princeton University Press, 1960). Kahn responded to the criticism of his strategic speculations with another polemical book, *Thinking About the Unthinkable* (New York: Avon Books, 1966). In his view, the criticisms of his adversaries were nothing but expressions of "Victorian prudery" (p. 20). It is difficult to determine to what extent his judgment is correct; but it is quite certain that Kahn is completely lacking not only in any kind of "prudery," Victorian or other, but also in any kind of regard for the destiny of those who for one reason or another dissent from the *pax americana* that he proposes. The language

97

Kahn uses has no precedents in the long and lugubrious history of intellectuals in the service of power. Even among the philosophers who backed fascist and Nazi totalitarianism (and we are not referring to Alfred Rosenberg, but rather to names of quality, such as Giovanni Gentile and Carl Schmitt), we find no one who dared speak as clearly as Kahn has done. See Jean-Pierre Faye, "Langages totalitaires—fascistes et nazis" in *Cahiers Internationaux de Sociologie*, 36 (1964), 75–100. It is a curious development: Theodore Roosevelt used to call things by name; he disliked masking the imperialistic actions of his country. The politicians of today prefer instead to present their adventures as international policemen as genuine crusades of democratic altruism; but the intellectuals who aid or counsel them do not care to accompany them in these semantic manipulations. Kahn today is just as explicit as Roosevelt was at the beginning of the century. He too calls things by their names, using the uneuphemistic language of the "big stick policy." He reconfirms that attitude in his book *The Year 2000* (New York: Macmillan, 1967). It is supposed to be an objective document forecasting the future; but in fact, it offers us a version of a future world seen exclusively through the imperialistic eyes of a great power. His models ("scenarios") of economic, political, technical, and military prediction are based on the methodological abstraction of "surprise-free requirements"—that is to say, on the presupposition that the "trends" that exist today will continue to develop tomorrow exactly according to the same index of increase or decrease functioning today. The future of the technical apparatus is judged mainly on the basis of its adaptability to the diplo-military needs of the great power in question: for its effectiveness in "a future 'Vietnam' or domestic trouble spot" (p. 97), or for its contribution "to help [militarily] the indigenous government" (p. 81). Another very influential personality is Henry Kissinger, who is currently Assistant for National Security Affairs in Washington. His two recent books, *Nuclear Weapons and Foreign Policy* (New York: Council on Foreign Relations–Harper & Row, 1957), and *The Necessity for Choice: Prospects of American Foreign Policy* (New York: Harper & Row, 1961), are substantially not very different from Kahn's works. Nevertheless, in his book *The Troubled Partnership: A Reappraisal of the Atlantic Alliance* (New York: Council on Foreign Relations–McGraw-Hill, 1965), a more open and realistic attitude is discernible.

7. In fact, McNamara has represented a rather exceptional phenomenon among the "new utopians": they usually prefer to play their role in the protective shadow of power, rather than play the more dangerous role of wielding power itself. McNamara not only accepted power, but aspired to absolute "leadership" in his area. Moreover, McNamara's approach had nothing in common with the traditional approach of intellectuals who get close to power: he wanted to be neither a *chroniqueur* nor a "man of culture in government." McNamara is not Malraux. For Malraux, power was really just one more adventure, the last stage in a long journey that had brought him through "the world of mind and fiction, which is the world of the artists, then through the world of struggle into the world of history"—*Antimemoirs* (New York: Holt, Rinehart and Winston, 1968). Like all intellectuals in a similar situation, Malraux strove to make us understand that "the truth of a man is first of all that which he hides"—*ibid.* He would have us catch a glimpse of the other Malraux behind the "Malraux-minister," the one who suffered in the situation to which his thirst for adventure had brought him. In McNamara we find no reservations of that sort. The technician in power, the technocrat, represents a new phase in the long and complex history of the relationships between intellectuals and the power structures. Perhaps the most acute and, for its time, prophetic description of the social profile of the technocrat of today was furnished by Antonio Gramsci, in about 1930, when he was trying to define that personage he defined generally as the "urban intellectual." In his book *Gli intellettuali e l'organizzazione della cultura* (Turin: Einaudi, 1966), he wrote: "Intellectuals of the urban type grew together with industry, are linked to its fortunes. . . . On the average, urban intellectuals are very standardized; the high urban intellectuals are fusing ever more with the real industrial general staff" (p. 10). "It comes about that many intellectuals think they are the State; a belief which, given

99

the impressive mass of the category, sometimes has notable consequences, and brings about unpleasant complications for the
basic economic group that *really* is the State." (p. 12). As we
can see, Gramsci recognized clearly the strong role of the intellectual in the industrial power structure, and, on the other hand, his
relative impotence when he tries to get too close to real direction
of the state. On the role of technicians in capitalist and even
socialist society, judgments have generally been far too summary.
In our opinion, that is a criticism that can be made even of the
book by Theodore Roszak, *The Making of a Counter Culture—
Reflections on the Technocratic Society and its Youthful Opposition* (New York: Doubleday, 1969), which from many points
of view is an example of analytical rigor and finesse. One of the
few authors who has perceived the nuances of the technocratic
phenomenon is Alain Touraine. In his book *Le mouvement de
Mai ou le Communisme utopique* (Paris: Editions du Seuil, 1969),
p. 16, the Nanterre sociologist emphasized the need for dis-
tinguishing between "technocratic ideology" and "technocratic
action." The first leads to a "negation of politics, reduced to
science, as if the choice of objectives and of values could be completely suppressed by the search for a rational concatenation of
means." The second, instead, "is in the service of the power of
the production apparatus, which it identifies with the general
progress of society."

8. Robert McNamara, *The Essence of Security: Reflections in
Office* (New York: Harper & Row, 1968).

9. Stewart Alsop, *The Center: The Anatomy of Power in
Washington* (New York: Harper & Row, 1968). On McNamara
as a representative of "the coolest of cool rationalism," see H.
Brandon, *Anatomy of Error: The Inside Story of the Asian War
on the Potomac: 1954–1969* (Boston: Gambit, 1969).

10. Virginia Held, "PPBS Comes to Washington," *The Public
Interest*, 4 (Summer, 1966), 102–15.

11. That is the thesis maintained by Anatol Rapoport in his
excellent book, *Strategy and Conscience* (New York: Harper &
Row, 1964): "The Good-Evil dichotomy nourishes the Devil
image. The Devil image justifies the model of current history

as an apocalyptic struggle. This being the age of science, not only technology but also scientific modes of thought must be mobilized in the conduct of the struggle. Hence the hegemony of strategic thinking in international affairs and the impasse which results from exclusive reliance on it" (p. 201).

12. John Kenneth Galbraith, *The New Industrial State* (New York: New American Library, 1968).

13. Antonio Gramsci, *Gli intellettuali*, p. 11.

14. Dieter Senghaas, "Sozialkybernetik und Herrschaft," *Atomzeitalter*, 7–8 (July-August, 1967). In reality, there are important precursors of that new view among those who for some years have tried to make a radical distinction between "national security research" and "peace research." On this subject, see K. E. Boulding, "Reality Testing and Value Orientation in International Systems: The Role of Research," *International Social Journal*, 17:3 (1965), 404–16. See the book by Frances Fornari, *Dissacrazione della guerra* (Milan: Feltrinelli, 1969); and also Dieter Senghaas, *Aggressivität und Gewalt-Thesen zur Abschreckungspolitik*; Herbert Marcuse et al., *Aggression und Anpassung in der Industriegesellschaft* (Frankfurt: Suhrkamp Verlag, 1968), pp. 128*ff*.

Chapter Five

1. The expression "megastructures" is used here for convenience of language. We are quite aware that we are rather arbitrarily grouping under this term a family of very vast and diversified architectonic and urbanistic proposals. For us, "megastructures" are the "Walking City" of Ron Herron and Bryan Harvey, the "Computer City" of Dennis Crompton, the "Plug-in City" of W. Chalk, P. Cook, and Dennis Crompton, the "Ville Cybernétique" of Nicolas Schöffer, the "Metabolist Structure" of Arata Isozaki, the "Ville Mobile–Ville Spatiale" of Yona Friedman, the "Helicoidal City" of Noriaki Kurokawa, the "Isotopon" of Rudolph Doernach. For some years, Banham's "gloriously technicolorful prose," as it was once described by one of his youthful admirers in the review *Clip-Kit*, has played a role in the diffusion

of the English current of this movement. See P. R. Banham, "A Clip on Architecture," *Design Quarterly*, 63 (1965). Historical precedents of this movement might be sought in Antonio Sant'-Elia, Kurt Schwitters, Bruno Taut, and Ivan Leonidov; nevertheless such genealogies are not very enlightening and perhaps not even very true. The most accurate description of "megastructuralism" is that of D. Scott Brown in his essay, "Little Magazines in Architecture and Urbanism," *Journal of the American Institute of Planners*, 34:4 (July, 1968). "The Futurist movement was said to represent the 'union of the psyche with horsepower'; here, now, is its union with rocketry—via Buckminster Fuller, Detroit, industrial gadgetry of the space program, package technology, computers, science fiction, and the science fiction comics" (p. 225). "A final theme is Fun. Here their location in the England of the Beatles is important, for they combine two enthusiasms: one for the up and swinging mass-pop culture of teenage London, and the other for the mass-pop packaged, engineering, expertise cult of industrial product technology" (p. 227). "Many of the cities do look familiar. They look like the industrial outskirts of American cities; like Jersey tank farms and cracking towers, or the oil derricks, pumps and cranes of San Pedro harbor, and the Huntington Beach sections of California's Route 1. One may question whether theirs is not, in fact, a nineteenth century rather than a late twentieth century industrial vision" (p. 230).

2. Fuller, 'The Year 2000," *Architectural Design* (February, 1967), p. 63.

3. Fuller, *Education Automation* (Illinois: Southern Illinois University Press, 1962), p. 76.

4. In the book *Utopia or Oblivion* (London: Allen Lane, The Penguin Press, 1970), R. Buckminster Fuller writes: "Politicians are not scientific inventors. The invention and system-design revolution must come before the political adjustments. Revolution by design and invention is the only revolution tolerable to all men, all societies, and all political systems anywhere" (p. 236).

5. *The Year 2000*, p. 76.

6. C. Wright Mills, *The Sociological Imagination* (New York: Grove Press [Evergreen Edition], 1961), p. 5.

CHAPTER SIX

1. In traditional demography, "population is the sum total of all people living within the confines of a given area." The appearance of "paleodemography" has considerably enriched this original notion. Having to determine the number and density of populations now disappeared, that is to say, of "people who lived within a determined area" in past ages, it has had to have recourse to the indirect procedure of establishing the number and the density of the "artifacts" that men used. The reason is that objects resist the action of time better than human remains do. See C. S. Coon and E. E. Hunt Jr., *Anthropology* (New York: Grosset & Dunlap, 1963), pp. 38*ff.* Methodological exigencies have brought this approach to recognize objects too as components of population. Moreover, ecologists have long considered "populations" to be groupings of every type of organism. See G. L. Clarke, *Elements of Ecology*, particularly the notion of the "ecology of population." As a matter of fact, ecologists have developed "demoecology." This new branch of ecology (or more precisely, of senecology) was defined by an Italian scholar as follows: "Demoecology is concerned with the study of uni- or intra-specific populations, conceived of in the abstract, or examined in the laboratory or even in their environment; or with the study of their peculiar characteristics, of their dynamics, the exchanges of energy with the external world, and with the relationships among the populations themselves and the communities, which are nothing but the entirety of populations belonging to several species"—Giorgio Marcuzzi, *Ecologia animale* (Milan: Feltrinelli, 1968), p. 15. A greater and even more audacious extrapolation of the concept of population comes from the recent contribution of scholars inspired by cybernetics. A typical example is Abraham Moles, who considers that all entities of any nature can constitute a population if they obey certain conditions. This radical way of looking at things enables him to speak even of a "demography of objects" and of a "sociology of objects." In our opinion, Moles treated this subject most exhaustively in "Objet et communication," in *Communications*, 13 (1969). "A theory of objects of a sociological

103

character must be based first of all upon an analysis of that which exists. It will seek to construct a demography in the etymological sense of description of populations and of their variations—a term which we shall frequently substitute with park of objects. Such a study can lead to the complete universe of objects, or to defined species; and that poses the problem of a typology and of a classification of objects" (p. 10). "The phrase 'sociology of objects' is perfectly fitting from an etymological point of view: *Socius* derives from *sequor*, to follow, to accompany. Nothing there indicates explicitly that a society or a *socius* must necessarily be constituted by human beings" (p. 12). In an earlier article, "Notions de quantité en cybernétique," in *Les Etudes Philosophiques*, 2 (April-June, 1961), Moles had already spoken of a "demography of acts." In the typology of populations, we must not forget the meta-population—that is, the population of the relationships between the different populations. Obviously, that particular population whose components are not persons, things, actions, processes, etc., but rather the relationships between them, is also the most complex from the structural and functional point of view. R. S. Studer writes on this point: "This complexity is a natural outgrowth of more people emitting more complex behaviours; more communications; more knowledge about what is required; and more means for finding solutions"— "On Environmental Programming," *Arena Architectural Association Journal* (May, 1966), pp. 290–96.

CHAPTER SEVEN

1. John Davy, "Vous avez pourri la planète," in *Le Nouvel Observateur* (November 25, 1968), 26–30. Concerning the increase in the population of automobiles, the figures mentioned by *Architectural Forum* (June, 1965) are interesting: "At the current 1965 rate of production, Detroit will manufacture, on every single working day, a line of automobiles 140 miles (240 km) long, bumper to bumper. Hence, in approximately three weeks the line would stretch from New York to Los Angeles" (p. 65). For European readers, we can say that a direct line from Milan to Rome would

be covered in two days' production, and between Paris and Munich in three days' production.

2. Cited by Evert Clark, "Fast Jetport Action Is Urged by Javits," in *The New York Times* (December 22, 1966). In the past two years, air-traffic problems in the United States have become even worse.

3. From 1890 to 1910, the "theory of collapse" (*Zusammen-bruchstheorie*) was one of the most debated subjects among the various tendencies in Marxian hermeneutics. Lucio Colletti, in his recent introduction to one of the works by Eduard Bernstein, *I presupposti e i componenti della socialdemocrazia* (Bari: Laterza, 1968) dealt with exceptional acumen with the various implications of this debate, above all the political and philosophical. There is one point, however, which Colletti presents in a rather ambiguous manner, and which might cause some not irrelevant misunder-standings. In a passage of his text (p. xviii), he expresses the opinion that for Marx, the inevitable collapse of capitalism would be the result of a fatal "historical tendency," whereas for Karl Kautsky, the phenomenon takes place according to a fatal "natural necessity." A comparative analysis of texts by Marx and Kautsky on this point does not bear out that assertion. Although Kautsky did speak of "natural necessity" (*Naturnotwendigkeit*) in *Das Erfurter Programm* (Stuttgart: Verlag J. H. W. Diek Nacht, 1908), p. 106, Marx expresses himself in a very similar manner. In *Das Kapital, Werke* (Stuttgart: Cotta Verlag, 1962) IV, p. 925, Marx writes: "Capitalist production produces its own negation with the necessity of a process of nature (*mit der Notwendigkeit eines Naturprozesses*). It is the negation of negation." As we can see, Marx's Hegelian historicist vocabulary does not successfully hide his naturalistic fatalism.

CHAPTER EIGHT

1. Gore Vidal calls the ideological fatalism of the "happy end-ing" variety the "spirit of yet." Vidal, *Reflections Upon a Sinking Ship* (Boston: Little, Brown and Co., 1969), p. x. In English, the word "yet" means, among other things, "the possibility of sub-

sequent change, where there is still time." And Vidal reminds us that "optimists are great 'yet' users."

2. "In recent years, therefore, the expressed alarm at human misuse of stock resources has moderated. But previous misgivings concerning stock resources have been replaced with concern over other portions of the spectrum: resources which are renewable. The renewable resources, sometimes called life-cycle or fluid resources, are those which continually replenish themselves in the course of nature. They include air, water, soil, and all living organisms such as trees, grass, and animals. Human activity can aid in the replenishing process, but sometimes no replenishment is possible"—Earl F. Murphy, *Governing Nature* (Chicago: Quadrangle Books, 1967), p. 31.

3. Not a few of our disquieting states of "explosive congestion" are also due to the fact that we want to use more things than we produce, and we consume—in the real and proper sense—fewer than those we use. See Murphy, *Governing Nature*, who analyzes this phenomenon with great perspicacity. "The nineteenth century has traditionally been called an age of production and the twentieth an age of consumption. . . . Whatever insights may be gained from this, the larger problem, so far as resources are concerned, is that in both centuries man had been a user more than either a producer or a consumer. Mountains of junk demonstrate that modern urban industrial man does not consume autos, furniture, or appliances. That he does not consume even his food, fuel, and water is perhaps less obvious. He uses these things, extracts energy, changes the form, and then deludes himself into believing that the residues disappear. To push used matter to one side, to bury it, to flush it, or to blow it away on the winds is thought to constitute disposal. Men have assumed that there was a direct line from production to consumption to disappearance. Now it is evident that man, whether as producer or consumer, is part of a cycle. The residue streaming from his production and consumption do *not* disappear, and when they accumulate beyond a certain point, they very plainly demand reconsideration" (pp. 118*ff.*).

CHAPTER NINE

1. See Serge Chermayeff and Christopher Alexander, *Community and Privacy* (Garden City, N.Y.: Doubleday Anchor Books, 1965), pp. 46*ff*.

2. Adolphe Portmann, "Die Ordnungen des Lebendigen im Deutungsversuch der Biologie," in *Aspekte des Lebendigen* (Freiburg: Herder Bücherei, 1962), 184*ff*. The French-American biologist René Dubos, in *So Human an Animal* (New York: Scribner's, 1968), warns against the danger of believing that man continually adapts himself to new conditions: "Any discussion of the future must take into account the inexorable biological limitations of homo sapiens" (p. 28).

3. With regard to the difficulties and the psychophysiological implications of such an artificialization of the environment, see G. Melvill Jones, "From Land to Space in a Generation: An Evolutionary Challenge," in *Aerospatial Medicine* 39:12 (December, 1968), 1271–82.

4. Patrick Geddes, *Cities in Evolution* (London: E. Benn, 1968), p. 73.

CHAPTER TEN

1. On "posthistoric" man, see Lewis Mumford, *The Transformation of Man* (New York: Collier Books, 1962), pp. 117*ff*. On "postideological" man, see Daniel Bell, *The End of Ideology* (New York: The Free Press, 1962). On "postalphabetized" man, see Marshall McLuhan, *The Gutenberg Galaxy* (Toronto: University of Toronto Press, 1962).

2. Hannah Arendt, *The Human Condition* (New York: Doubleday Anchor Books, 1959).

3. Donald A. Schon, *Technology and Change—The New Heraclitus* (New York: Delacorte Press, 1967), pp. 20 and 25. For a complete presentation of the "risk-uncertainty" relationship, especially in the field of economics, see the book edited by Karl Borch and Jan Mossin, *Risk and Uncertainty, Proceedings of a Conference Held by the International Economic Association* (New York: St. Martin's Press, 1968).

107

4. On the subject of the relationship between science and design, in particular on the tendency to present too unilateral and simplistic a version thereof, see our article (in collaboration with Gui Bonsiepe) "Wissenschaft und Gestaltung," in *Ulm, Zeitschrift der Hochschule für Gestaltung,* 10–11 (May, 1964), 10–19.

5. The classification of problems as "well defined" and "ill defined" is fundamental. The first systematic attempt to establish the nature of "well-defined problems" and to indicate the techniques most suitable for treating them was made by Marvin Minsky in his essay "Steps Toward Artificial Intelligence," in *Proceedings of the Institute of Radio Engineers,* 49 (January, 1961), pp. 8-30. But the limits between "well-defined" and "ill-defined" problems were fixed by W. R. Reitman in his article "Heuristic Decision Procedures, Open Constraints and the Structure of the Ill Defined Problem," in *Human Judgments and Optimality,* eds. W. M. Shelley and G. I. Bryan (New York: John Wiley, 1965).

6. Warren Weaver, "Science and Complexity," in *American Scientist,* 36 (1948), 536–44.

CHAPTER ELEVEN

1. "Suboptimization," as L. W. Hein defines it, "is the optimization of a part of the organization at the expense of the whole." *The Quantitative Approach to Managerial Decisions* (Englewood Cliffs, N.J.: Prentice-Hall, 1967), p. 2.

2. R. Buckminster Fuller, "Why No Roofs over Our Cities," in *Think* (January-February, 1968), 8–11. Inspired by the "great skylighted arcades of Milan," Buckminster Fuller conceived of a gigantic "domed-over" New York. "Such a cupola," he says, "would go from the East River to the Hudson River, with 42nd Street as its east-west axis, and its north-south axis going from 64th to 22nd Streets. It would consist of a hemisphere two miles in diameter, and a height of one mile at its center . . . an umbrella over it." On Fuller's geodesic domes, see Sibyl Moholy-Nagy, *Matrix of Man: An Illustrated History of Urban Environment* (London: The Pall Mall Press, 1968), p. 13.

3. Donovan Bess, "What the Space Scientists Propose for Cali-

fornia," in *Think*, 32:4 (July-August, 1969). On the same subject, see W. L. Rogers, "Aerospace Systems Technology and the Creation of Environment," in *Environment for Man*, ed. W. R. Ewald (Bloomington, Ind.: Indiana University Press, 1967), pp. 260*ff*.

4. Is it right to say that deurbanization implies desocialization? Certainly it is so in this particular case. In the reality hypothesized here, work (which is now "domestic work") ends by domesticating the worker. All of a sudden nearly the whole of his communicative life is forced to unfold in the narrow social space of his individual domicile. The worker, white-collar or proletarian, is condemned to suffocating isolation. It is an isolation *en famille*, but it is still isolation. His real relationships with other men are reduced to a minimum. The television screen, which used to exist only as a function of entertainment, now appears, as monitor, as a function of work. The world of others is no longer at arm's length, but now only within reach of the television screen. And thus society empties itself of all tangible concreteness. It becomes spectral. Work itself, in the worker's eyes and in the eyes of others, also becomes spectral; it loses its social identity. In the end it is desocialized. In less extreme cases, however, the causal dependence between deurbanization and desocialization is more difficult to establish. Usually, any effort in this direction is mired down in the old problem of the city versus the country. As we will remember, the problem does not at first present itself with the characteristics that we attribute to it today. In the first phase, it appears exclusively as a polemic against the city. The most illustrious supporter of that view was Jean-Jacques Rousseau. "Men," writes Rousseau, "are not made to be piled up in ant hills, but to live scattered on the earth they must cultivate. The more they get together, the more they corrupt each other. The diseases of the body, like the vices of the soul, are the inevitable consequences of being grouped together in numbers far too large. Of all the animals, man is the least successful in living in groups. Men herded together like so many sheep would all die in a short time. The breath of man is fatal to his fellow men: and that is true both in the figurative and the real sense." Jean-Jacques Rousseau, *Emile* in *Oeuvres Complètes* (Paris: Gallimard, Bibliothèque de

la Pléiade, 1969) IV, p. 276. Paradoxically enough, this attitude against the city has had a profound influence in the country that created the most ambitious urban settlements in history, the United States. ". . . Dismay and distrust have been the predominant attitudes of the American intellectual toward the American city"—M. White, "The Philosopher and the Metropolis in America," in *Urban Life and Form*, ed. W. Z. Hirsch (New York: Holt, Rinehart and Winston, 1965). See also M. and L. White, *The Intellectual versus the City—From Thomas Jefferson to Frank Lloyd Wright* (New York: New American Library, 1964). The polemic against the city and in defense of an idealized nature reached its apogee in the nineteenth century and the beginning of the twentieth century. In the 1920s, interest in the subject declined. Little by little, the modern city as it had developed during capitalism begins to be considered an irreversible evil. Many resign themselves; others, more stubborn, seek refuge among the conservationists. As a result of the tendency to blame the city alone for every ecological catastrophe, there is discernible today a re-emergence of the traditional Rousseauan attitude, now perhaps more violent than before. It is opposed by a position that defends the city at all costs: even at the cost of good sense and good faith. The best example thereof is the last book by Jane Jacobs, *The Economy of Cities* (New York: Random House, 1969). It is an extreme effort on the part of American liberalism to justify the calamitous dysfunction of the city of today. An attempt to demonstrate that precisely because of these dysfunctions the city is able to regenerate itself spontaneously. It is once again the ideology of the "happy ending" we mentioned earlier. Curiously enough, we find the return here of the slogan "the worse it gets, the better," which belongs to the line of reasoning of the opposite tendency, to the preachers of the "unhappy ending." But this time it is used in the name of goodnatured liberal optimism: the worse the city develops, the greater becomes the economic dynamic of the urban system, and the greater becomes the possibility of its salvation. Here are some quotations from the book by Jacobs: "People who think we would be better off without cities, especially without big, unmanageable, disorderly cities, never tire of explaining that cities grown too big are, in any case, inefficient and impractical [p. 85]. . . . But I propose to argue that these grave and real deficiencies are necessary to economic development and thus are exactly what make cities uniquely valuable to economic life. By this, I do not mean that cities are economically valuable in spite of their inefficiency and impracticality but rather because they are inefficient and impractical . . . [p. 86]." The statement is of an olympian explicitness. Nothing is hidden. Everything is understandable. And what we understand is truly unusual. In the final analysis, according to this way of seeing things, the important thing is not so much the physical and mental health of men who live in "inefficient and impractical" cities; for Jacobs, the only important thing is economic development. In this age of open rebellion against all traditional stereotypes of thought, it is moving to find such a pure, barely disguised expression of traditional bourgeois economic sentiments. It is obvious, however, that the debate on the city, carried on in such abstractly generic terms, cannot but lead into a blind alley. In such a context, the relationship between deurbanization and desocialization can never be clarified in a convincing manner. The problem of the city versus the country goes beyond the conflict between urbanophiles and urbanophobes, and between supporters and enemies of the city. Here we need to examine another viewpoint that has developed somewhat at the margin of this conflict. We are alluding to the view implicit in the dispute that has arisen among Marxists concerning the modalities for carrying out the socialist territorial installation. The precedents of this debate go back to Marx and Engels. Their violent indictment in 1845 of the capitalist city-country antinomy is well known. According to them, that antinomy would force mankind to become either a "narrow-minded city animal" (borniertes Stadttier) or a "narrow-minded country animal" (borniertes Landtier). It should be pointed out, however, that it was precisely Marx and Engels who, on that very occasion, were the first to indicate the complexity of the city-country problem, and the first to warn against the dangers of simplistic and miracle-working prescriptions. "The overcoming of the opposition

111

between city and country is one of the primary conditions for society, a condition that still depends on a mass of material presuppositions, and which pure will cannot satisfy, as anyone can see at first glance. These conditions have still to be developed." Karl Marx and Friedrich Engels, *Die deutsche Ideologie* (Moscow and Leningrad: MEGA, Erste Abteilung, V, Verlagsgenossenschaft ausländischer Arbeiter in der UdSSR, 1932–33), pp. 39ff. Later, in the *Anti-Dühring*, Engels develops his often misunderstood theory of the "homogenous distribution" of big industry once again without forgetting to call attention to the difficulties that must be faced in bringing it about. "With the big cities, civilization has passed on to us an inheritance that will take great time and energy to eliminate." Friedrich Engels, *Anti-Dühring: Herr Eugen Dühring's Revolution in Science* (Moscow: Foreign Language Publishing House, 1962). Certainly, with the help of "pure will" (*blosse Wille*) and without a profound examination of the "material presuppositions" (*materielle Voraussetzungen*) that can make it possible, the proposal of a "homogeneous distribution" appears to be, if not utopia, at least an ideal construct. We must not forget that the proposal aims at nothing less than a fusion (or hybridization) of city and country, that is to say, it seeks to oppose an urban socialist continuity to an urban capitalist discontinuity. Still, several years before the *Anti-Dühring*, Engels had already denounced as petit bourgeois reformers those who see in the idea of fusion only a utopian whim. (See his famous polemic with Proudhon, Sax, and above all Müllberger in *Zur Wohnungsfrage, erstes Heft* (Verlag der Expedition des "Volksstaat"), *zweites und drittes Heft* (Leipzig: Verlag der Genossenschaftsbuchdruckerei, 1872). In short, the founders of Marxism were opposed both to the excessive simplifications of the voluntarism of the left, and the excessive caution of the reformism of the right. That is why the dispute among Marxists on the future of the city-country relationship has always presented itself as a conflict between voluntarists and reformers, or rather, as a permanent, mutual accusation of being voluntarists or reformers. And yet, there is a surprising fact: This dispute has not always been conditioned by the interpretative formulations of Marx and Engels.

For example, the conception of a "linear city" which was originally not Marxist but more likely inspired by Hausmann has also had a decisive influence in this context. Here too we have a proposal to fuse city and country, but very different from the earlier one. This time the fusion is conceived of in terms of a radical transformation of the physical structures, and not, as was the case with Marx and Engels, in terms of a radical transformation of society. One of the pioneers of the "linear city," the Spanish engineer Arturo Soria y Mata, wrote in 1882: "It is therefore a universal need, urgent beyond any other consideration, to reconcile the benefits and to suppress the disadvantages of rural life and urban life. To ruralize urban life, and to urbanize the countryside. That is the problem, and its solution today consists in the linear city"—"La ciudad lineal," in *El Progreso* (10:4, 1882). Reprinted in "Hogar y Arquitectura," 63 (March-April, 1966), 61. The "linear city" of Soria was the first attempt to express visually—that is, physically—a particular way of interpreting the fusion of city and country. Others followed, as is well known. We recall, for example, the projects for urban settlements on a continuous line, by Le Corbusier (1930), R. Neutra (1923–30), Frank Lloyd Wright (1934–35), L. Hilbersheimer (1944), and Kenzo Tange (1960). But it is in the Soviet Union at the end of the 1920s that the idea of a "linear city" assumes true theoretical and practical significance. In that period, it was the center of the controversy between voluntarist "deurbanists" who proposed it (M. Baršč, M. Ginzburg, M. Ochitovič, N. Sokolov, and A. L. Pasternak), and the "urbanist" reformers who opposed it. See L. M. Sabsovič et al., *La costruzione della città sovietica 1929–31*, ed. P. Ceccarelli (Padua: Marsilio, 1970); Anatole Kopp, *Town and Revolution: Soviet Architecture 1917–1935* (New York: Braziller, 1970); V. DeFeo, *URSS Architettura 1917–1936* (Rome: Editori Riuniti, 1963); V. Quilici, *L'architettura del costruttivismo* (Bari: Laterza, 1969). The winners of the contest were the reformers, which is to say, the realists, the cautious ones. As for the reasons for their victory, very diverse (and opposed) guesses have been hazarded. Personally, we are inclined to accept the thesis suggested by Ceccarelli in his excellent introduction to *La*

113

costruzione della città sovietica 1929–31, i.e., that neither the winners nor the losers were right in a general historical sense. But nevertheless, in the historical context of the Soviet Union of that time, the winners were able to offer an operatively feasible program, whereas their opponents were not. Or at least, the program they had worked out, despite the efforts of Miljutin, could not persuade the experts, who from the very beginning had denounced the superficial, arbitrary, and adventurous nature of its presuppositions. Obviously, it was not enough to proclaim deurbanization. They had to show how one could practicably begin a process of deurbanization in the framework of a socialist state under construction. Or rather, they had to give an answer to the very concrete question of how to reconcile this process with the unpostponable needs of the other developmental processes in society as a whole. The answer was not forthcoming. Nor did there prove to be anything in the hope of eliminating the ambiguities in the concept of deurbanization. It will be remembered that the oscillation in the meaning of this concept had caused many misunderstandings, even among the very defenders of the "linear city" (see the exchange of letters between Le Corbusier and the Soviet architect Ginzburg in 1930). The time that has passed since then has certainly not contributed to a clarification of the issue. Its meaning becomes ever more elusive. In an age like ours, an age of massive urbanization, the idea of deurbanization seems ungraspable. Even more, it seems to go against common sense. For many scholars, particularly for the Marxists, the word deurbanization seems compromising today. It is not worthwhile, they say, to sacrifice the destiny of an idea to the word that is used to express it. And they are right. Because when all is said and done, behind it there is nothing but the well-known phenomenon of the spatial decentralization of urban settlements. We will not deny that the word decentralization is somewhat ambiguous too, for in fact, decentralization is a tendency we encounter today both in capitalist and in socialist societies. But the ambiguity is not insuperable. There is a fundamental difference between capitalist and socialist decentralization. In the first, decentralization is only megalopolizing, i.e., the transferral to a territorial scale of the same procedures of desocialization broadly practiced on the scale of cities and even of neighborhoods; but in the second, decentralization is—or should be—the articulation of infrastructures as a function of a greater, more intense, richer, and more efficient socialization. And yet we ought to recognize that in socialist society, the technical-organizational premises for complete socialization are not completely evident. [See A. Gorz, *Le socialisme difficile* (Paris: Editions du Seuil, 1967).] Absolute socialization would presuppose an absolute homogenization of the roles of individuals in society—in other words, a definite overcoming of the division of labor, of the specialization of tasks. In line with that, every individual would be at once an intellectual, a worker, and a peasant; he would be at once an intellectual and a manual laborer. From an ideal point of view, there is nothing to be said against that. But in practice, we must admit that all efforts in that direction have met with insurmountable difficulties. The attempt has been made to impose suddenly a radical "superstructural" change, to speed the times toward a new "civil society." The results have been rather modest, and even negative. For the little that has been obtained, the "social cost" paid has been immense. Grave "superstructural" imbalances have been created (operative dysfunctions in institutions, human frustrations in individuals). That cannot help but have consequences. The "superstructural" imbalances, on their side, have caused "structural" insufficiencies that are equally grave (production goals not reached, and general slowdown in the plans for a socialist reconversion of the agrarian and industrial economy). The fact is, one has to move very cautiously with superstructures. Without doubt, it is much easier to proclaim "polyvalent man" than to realize him. It is true that the ideal of polyvalent man—in the Renaissance they called him the "universal man"—is a great old humanistic ideal. With one innovation: today, *all* men are to be polyvalent, and not just a privileged group. Which is an even more ambitious ideal. Nevertheless, historical experience shows that the more ambitious our ideals, the greater becomes the risk of "missing the mark," and of being thrown back to a state more precarious than the one in which we started out. For that reason, the farther our program aims, the more rigorous must be its foundation. The "polyvalent man," who is presented to us as the presupposition of the socialist fusion of city and country, is a model still to be precisely defined. Not only from the point of view of Marxist philosophical anthropology, but also from the point of view of socialist planning. The polyvalent man is nothing but the result of a professional availability, mobility, and functioning, preceded of course by an education oriented toward versatility rather than specialization. But if we set it up that way, the argument is still too generic, and quite far removed from being a technical argument. Pity that the recent resuscitation of the question of fusing city and country still insists on moving in this direction. See G. Dato et al., "Città del capitale e territorio socialista," in *Ideologie*, 9–10 (1969).

CHAPTER TWELVE

1. Nicolai Hartmann, "Systematische Methode," in *Logos*, 3 (1912), 121–63.

2. Ludwig von Bertalanffy, "General System Theory," in *General Systems, Yearbook of the Society for the Advancement of General Systems Research*, 7 (1962), 1–20. Reprinted in *Modern Systems Research for the Behavioral Scientist*, eds. Walter Buckley and Anatol Rapoport (Chicago: Aldine Publishing Co., 1968), pp. 11*ff*. Further, see, "General Theory of Systems: Applications to Psychology," in *The Social Sciences—Problems and Orientations* (The Hague–Paris: Mouton-Unesco, 1968), 309*ff*. Also, *General System Theory—Foundations, Development, Application* (New York: Braziller, 1969). The biological approach to the notion of system has been treated very accurately by J. C. Miller, "Living Systems: Basic Concepts," in *Behavioral Sciences* (July, 1965), 193–237.

3. In his essay, "La dissacrazione della guerra e i fondamenti della scienza," in *Dissacrazione della guerra*, Franco Fornari draws a distinction between intrasystemic, intersystemic, and trans-systemic. The first and second notions are acceptable, but the third is not. In our opinion, the possibility of transsystemic behavior is purely speculative.

4. C. Foster, Anatol Rapoport, and E. Trucco, "Some Unsolved Problems in the Theory of Non-Isolated Systems," in *General Systems, Yearbook of the Society for General Systems Research* 2 (1957), 9–29.

CHAPTER THIRTEEN

1. Vilfredo Pareto, *Trattato di sociologia generale* (Florence: Barbera, 1916).

2. Condillac, *Traité des systèmes* in *Oeuvres philosophiques de Condillac* (Paris: Presses Universitaires de France, 1951), III, pp. 511*ff*.

3. Talcott Parsons and E. A. Shils, *Toward a General Theory of Action* (Cambridge, Mass.: Harvard University Press, 1954). Cf. C. Wright Mills, *The Sociological Imagination*, pp. 25*ff*.

4. A. D. Hall, *A Methodology for Systems Engineering* (Princeton: Van Nostrand, 1962). "A system," says Hall, "is a set of objects with relationships between the objects and between their attributes" (p. 60). See the distinction he draws between a system as such and "external" system, which he calls "environment." "For a given system, the environment is the set of all objects outside the system, (1) a change in whose attributes affects the system, and (2) whose attributes are changed by the behavior of the system" (p. 61). "It is important to see that physical systems do not exist merely *in* an environment; they exist *by means* of an environment" (p. 62).

5. *Ibid.*, "Most physical systems change with time. If these changes lead to a gradual transition from wholeness to independence, the system is said to undergo *progressive* factorization. We can distinguish two kinds of progressive factorization. The first and simplest kind . . . corresponds to decay. It is as though, through much handling, the parts of a jigsaw puzzle become so rounded that a given piece no longer fits the other pieces better than another. Or suppose an automobile were deprived of maintenance. The engine would wear out, the tires would rot, and eventually the parts will no longer behave as a system. The second kind of progressive factorization corresponds to growth. The system changes in the direction of increasing division into

117

subsystems and subsubsystems, or differentiation of functions. This kind of factorization appears in systems involving some creative process, or in evolutionary and developmental processes" (pp. 65*ff.*).

6. Walter Buckley, *Sociology and Modern Systems Theory* (Englewood Cliffs, N.J.: Prentice-Hall, 1967), pp. 58*ff.*

7. Ruth Benedict, *Patterns of Culture* (New York: New American Library, 1946).

CHAPTER FOURTEEN

1. Hannah Arendt, *Über die Revolution* (Munich: Piper Verlag, 1963), pp. 333*ff.*

2. Rosa Luxemburg, *Organisationsfragen der russuschen Sozialdemokratie*, in *Politische Schriften*, ed. Ossip K. Flechtheim (Frankfurt: Europäische Verlagsanstalt, 1968), III, pp. 83*ff.* See also Peter Nettl, *Rosa Luxemburg* (Cologne and Berlin: Kiepenhauer Witsch, 1967).

3. Max Weber, "Die drei reinen Typen der legitimen Herrschaft" in *Soziologie, Weltgeschichtliche Analysen, Politik*, ed. J. Winckelmann (Stuttgart: Kronen Verlag, 1956), p. 151.

4. "Der Beruf zur Politik," *loc cit.*, p. 180.

5. Ernst Bloch, *Thomas Münzer als Theologe der Revolution* (Frankfurt: Suhrkamp Verlag, 1962).

6. Walter Benjamin, *Das Kunstwerk im Zeitalter seiner technischen Reproduzierbarkeit* (Frankfurt: Suhrkamp Verlag, 1963), pp. 48*ff.* "Fascism," writes Benjamin, "consistently tends toward an aestheticization of political life" (p. 48). "All efforts toward an aestheticization of politics converge at one point. That point is war" (p. 49).

CHAPTER FIFTEEN

1. Tom Wolfe, *The Kandy-Kolored Tangerine-Flake Streamline Baby.* By the same author, see also *The Electric Kool-Aid Acid Test* (New York: Farrar, Straus & Giroux, 1968). In this book, there are many vivid descriptions of other urban "landscapes" in the

United States, similar to those in Las Vegas. "One after another, electric signs with neon martini glasses lit up on them, the San Francisco symbol of 'bar'—thousands of neon-magenta martini glasses bouncing and streaming down the hill . . ." (p. 3). "The Life! A glorious place, a glorious age, I tell you. A very Neon Renaissance . . ." (p. 41). In reality, this is the same sort of ingenuous enthusiasm shown by Walt Whitman, Apollinaire, Marinetti, Blaise Cendrars, and Vladimir Majakowsky when they beheld the nascent world of the machine.

2. In fact, the attempt to make use of a semiotic set of ideas to describe communicative (and even aesthetic) phenomena in the fields of architecture, urbanistics, and "industrial design" have not yet yielded the results that many expected, for many reasons, but above all for the lack of maturity in the semiotic itself. The only truly well-articulated semiotic set of ideas is the one by Charles W. Morris. Although its origin, as is well known, is "behaviorist," it is not fair to reduce it only to that dimension, as has been done recently. We must remember that Morris's semiotics derive directly from C. S. Peirce, who was a genial interpreter and continuer of the best traditions in the philosophy of meaning, that is to say, of Aristotle, Sextus Empiricus, Petrus Hispanus, Duns Scotus, William of Occam, Leibniz, Augustus de Morgan, George Boole, W. S. Jevons, and many others. Morris was also very strongly influenced by currents of contemporary thought that have little or nothing to do with "behaviorism," for example, the neo-positivism of the *Wiener Kreis*, the logic of the Polish school, the pragmatism of John Dewey and A. F. Bentley, the philosophy of symbolic forms of Ernst Cassirer, the new rhetoric of I. A. Richards and C. K. Ogden, the incipient social psychology of G. H. Mead, and the linguistics of Ferdinand de Saussure. (For a criticism of Morris's "behaviorism," see the Introduction to our *Beitrag zur Terminologie der Semiotik* (Ulm: Korrelat, 1961). Morris was also the one who revealed the possibility of applying semiotics to the study of aesthetic phenomena. His principal contributions in this field are "Esthetics and the Theory of Signs (ETS)" in *Journal of Unified Science*, 8 (1939); and "Science, Art, and Technology" in *Kenyon Review*, 1:4 (Autumn, 1939). This is not the place to

discuss the problems of semiotic aesthetics; but it is important to point out that the difficulties encountered by all those who have tried to apply semiotics to the fields we mentioned were already encountered in these two essays by Morris. (For the current difficulty in the use of certain notions in Morris's semiotics, see the excellent essay by Ferruccio Rossi-Landi, "Significato, ideologia, e realismo artistico," in *Nuova Corrente*, 44 [1967], 300–42.) The definition of iconic sign still remains the major obstacle. Faced with "abstract art," that is to say, with art that by definition rejected iconicity, Morris was forced to present a more multifaceted, but also a weaker definition of iconic sign. Originally, in *ETS*, he had defined the work of art as a sign, more precisely as an iconic sign. But in *SAT*, he had to admit that the referent of an aesthetic iconic sign was a value, not an object. [On this point, see X. Rubert de Ventós, *Teoría de la sensibilidad* (Barcelona: Ediciones Península, 1969), p. 422.] The German philosopher Max Bense was one of the first in postwar Europe to try to use Morris's semiotics not only for an analysis of sign structures in works of art, but for industrial products as well—Max Bense, *Aesthetica I* (Stuttgart: Deutsche Verlagsanstalt, 1954); *Aesthetica II, Aesthetische Information* (Krefeld: Agis Verlag, 1956); *Aesthetica III, Aesthetik und Zivilisation* (Krefeld: Agis Verlag, 1958); *Aesthetica IV, Programmierung des Schönen* (Krefeld: Agis Verlag, 1960). Although Bense's attempt to found an aesthetic from both the perspective of semiotics and the theory of information has proved productive in many ways, it has not produced valid results with regard to the problem that concerns us here. The major difficulty has been Bense's obstinate refusal to break with the German Idealist tradition, and his insistence on working with the notion of Beauty. That is particularly inexplicable in someone who so frequently bases himself on the thought of C. S. Peirce. The great recluse of Mildford wrote: "That science [aesthetics] has been handicapped by the definition of it as the theory of beauty" —*Collected Papers of C. S. Peirce*, eds. C. Hartshorne and P. Weiss (Cambridge, Mass: The Belknap Press of Harvard University Press, 1960), II, p. 117. The other factor that has had a negative influence on Bense's promising approach has been the fact that his desire to "mathematicize beauty" has lead him to a sort of neo-Pythagoreanism, to something like an academic *Kompositionslehre* and *Proportionslehre*, presented with the semiotic-informational nomenclature and executed with the aid of computers. This tendency has taken on rather openly regressive features in his students and followers. In fact, it seems to be a return, by means of G. D. Birkhoff (whom they have misunderstood) to the most ingenuous simplifications of aesthetic phenomena and processes, typical of the "experimental" aesthetics of Theodor Fechner, Wilhelm Wundt, and Theodor Lipps. These experts in *Informationsaesthetik* consider all problems of preferential aesthetic behavior to be practically nonexistent, be they at the level of the individual, the group, or an entire culture. In other words, they have driven history and society into exile, without much compunction. See Rul Gunzenhäuser, *Aesthetisches Mass und aesthetische Information* (Quickborn bei Hamburg: Verlag Schnelle, 1962); Kurd Alsleben, *Aesthetische Redundanz* (Quickborn bei Hamburg: Verlag Schnelle, 1962); Rolf Garnich, *Konstruktion, Design, Aesthetik* (Esslingen am Neckar: Selbstverlag, Rolf Garnich, 1968). But the most clamorous example of this approach is surely the book by Manfred Kiemle, *Aesthetische Probleme der Architektur unter dem Aspekt der Informationsaesthetik* (Quickborn bei Hamburg: Verlag Schnelle, 1967). In Italy, interest in the logical-philosophical foundations of the problem has an important tradition, especially if we recall the monumental works of Giuseppe Peano. See Peano, *Formulario matematico* (Rome: Cremonese, 1960), and his *Opere scelte* (Rome: Cremonese, 1957–58–59). The diffusion of Morris's semiotic is the responsibility of Silvio Ceccato and above all of Ferruccio Rossi-Landi, who knows more about Morris's thought than just about anyone in Europe. Concern with the specific relationship between semiotics and architecture began in Italy in the proper way: as semantic criticism of the critical thought on architecture. That was the precise contribution made in the brilliant article by Sergio Bettini, "Critica semantica e continuita storica dell'architettura europea," in *Zodiac*, 2 (1958), 7–25. It was an effort, as Bettini himself defined it, "to overcome the noncriticability of architecture" (p.

18). In the general presentation of the relationship between semiotics and architecture, Gillo Dorfles's book *Il divenire delle arti* (Turin: Einaudi, 1959) played an important role; and even more important was his *Simbolo, communicazione e consumo* (Turin: Einaudi, 1962). Still in Italy, the application of Morris's set of ideas to an analysis of the foundations of architectural planning is the work of G. K. Koenig, *Analisi del linguaggio architettonico* (Florence: Libreria Editrice Fiorentina, 1964). (The book is based on the notes of a course given by Koenig in 1960–61.) After this contribution came many other publications, dealing with various aspects of the subject of architecture as language from varied points of view. See Cesare Brandi, *Struttura e architettura* (Turin: Einaudi, 1967); Renato de Fusco, *Architettura come mass-medium —note per una semiologia architettonica* (Bari: Dedalo Libri, 1967); Umberto Eco, *La struttura assente: Introduzione alla ricerca semiologica* (Milan: Bompiani, 1968); Renato de Fusco, *Tre contributi alla semiologia architettonica, op. cit.*, 12 (May, 1968); J. M. Rodriguez et al., *Architettura come semiotica* (Milan: Tamburini, 1968). The most meritorious effort to advance the question of semiotics and architecture is nevertheless represented, without doubt, by section C in the book by Eco. Generally, however, it can be said that nearly all these publications suffer from the very negative influence of the French school of semiology, which brought about a regression in a development of conceptualization that already possessed a relative coherence. See Françoise Choay, "Semiologie et urbanisme," in *Architecture d'aujourd'hui*, 38 (June–July, 1967), 8–10. Structuralist semiology, in my opinion, does not represent a step forward with respect to Morris, but rather a step backward, bringing the discussion back to the early and undoubtedly genial intuitions of Ferdinand de Saussure. One of the few interesting contributions of Roland Barthes to the problem that interests us here is the observation that to speak of "the language of the city" is a metaphorical abuse. Barthes is also right in appealing for a "passage from metaphor to a description of the sense," though he himself does not do it. See Roland Barthes, "Semiologia e urbanistica," *op. cit.*, 10 (September, 1967), 11. As a matter of fact when we spoke at the beginning of the modest results attained, we were referring precisely to this. The semiotics (or the semiology) of architecture still remains at the metaphorical level. It would seem that up to now, all efforts have been directed exclusively toward a substitution of the terminology for another, and little more. This may be clearly seen in the works of Brandi and De Fusco, in their obvious concern with the critical assimilation of certain components of the traditional interpretative categories of ideas of Heinrich Wölfflin and Erwin Panofsky into the new set of problems. See Heinrich Wölfflin, *Das Erklären von Kunstwerken* (Cologne: Verlag E. A. Seemann, 1940, first ed. 1921); and Erwin Panofsky, *Meaning in the Visual Arts* (New York: Doubleday, 1967). At times it is difficult to understand the difference between Wölfflin's *Formerklären* and Panofsky's "iconology" on the one hand, and current semiotic terminology used to interpret works of art on the other. For the moment, the difference resides mainly in words. The fact that the break with the earlier descriptive tradition is only of a terminological nature has led many supporters of the new approach to a rather inconsistent attitude. Christian Norberg-Schulz, for example, in his *Intentions in Architecture* (Rome: Universitetsforlaget, 1963), had seen with great acumen the importance of semiotics in critical discourse about architecture; but then he returned to the usage of very traditional historicist categories in his recent essay, "Il concetto di luogo," *Controspazio*, 1 (June, 1969), 20–23. For a criticism of the relationship between semiotics and architecture, see also Nuno Portas, *A Arquitectura para hoje* (Lisbon: Livraria Sá da Costa, 1964), pp. 110ff.

3. Robert Venturi and D. Scott Brown, "A Significance for A & P Parking Lots or Learning from Las Vegas," in *Architectural Forum*, 128:2 (March, 1968). On the same subject, see D. Scott Brown, "On Pop-Art, Permissiveness, and Planning," in *Journal of the American Institute of Planners*, 35:3 (May, 1969). And also C. Jencks, "Pop—Non Pop," in *Architectural Association Quarterly* (Winter, 1968–69), 48.

4. See our article "Neue Entwicklungen in der Industrie und die Ausbildung des Produktgestalters," in *Ulm*, 2 (October, 1958), 30. For the debate on this article, in which the participants were Bruno

Alfieri, Reyner Banham, Misha Black, Gillo Dorfles, Ettore Sottsass Jr., and Marco Zanuso, see *Stile Industria*, 21 (1959), pp. 21–25. The article by Banham alluded to here is "Industrial Design e arte populare," in *Civiltà delle macchine* (November-December, 1955). In this context, it might be profitable to read the Introduction by J. Eisen to the anthology *The Age of Rock—Sounds of the American Cultural Revolution* (Vintage Books, New York, 1969), which he also edited. Eisen writes: "The fifties marked the end of the divorce between 'art' for those at the top and 'circuses' for those at the bottom" (p. xii). But a little further on, when discussing the bitter critical observations made by Paul Johnson against "rock music," he is forced to recognize that "the entertainment industry and its satellites exist not to further the revolution, but to make money, and they exist largely through cultural debasement and the crassest form of exploitation. . . . They will respond to new popular desires as much as they create them" (p. xiii).

5. Venturi and Brown, "A Significance . . .," p. 91.

6. Amos Rapoport and R. E. Kantor, "Complexity and Ambiguity in Environmental Design," in *Journal of the American Institute of Planners*, 33:4 (July, 1967), 211.

7. Hy Day, "Attention, Curiosity, and Exploration," in *Design and Planning*, ed. M. Krampen (New York: Hasting House, 1965). In this article, Day discusses the experiments of D. E. Berlyne on the relationship between curiosity and complexity in visual perception. On the same subject, see D. E. Berlyne, *Conflict, Arousal and Curiosity* (New York: McGraw-Hill, 1960), pp. 18*ff*. Also by Berlyne, "Novelty and Curiosity as Determinants of Exploratory Behavior," in *British Journal of Psychology*, 41 (1950), 68–80; "Conflict and Information-Theory Variables as Determinants of Human Perceptual Curiosity," in *Journal of Experimental Psychology*, 53:6 (1967), 399–404; and "Complexity and Incongruity Variables as Determinants of Exploration Choice and Evaluate Ratings," in *Canadian Journal of Psychology*, 17:3 (1963), 274–90.

8. Karl Marx, *Zur Kritik der Nationalökonomie—Ökonomisch-philosophische Manuskripte*, p. 66.

9. Robert Venturi, *Complexity and Contradiction in Architecture* (Museum of Modern Art, New York, 1966), p. 23.

10. See our article "Problemas actuales de la comunicación" in *Nueva Visión*, 4 (1953), 21.

11. Samuel Taylor Coleridge, *Biographia Literaria*, ed. J. Shaveross (London: Oxford University Press, 1962), II, p. 255.

12. See Alan Solomon, "The New Art," in *The New Art*, ed. G. Battcock (New York: E. P. Dutton, 1966). Solomon observes: "They are tourists from another country, with resources and a spirit of curiosity which permit them to observe Disneyland with delight and amazement" (p. 75). "For whatever historical reasons, the new artists are detached politically (they have not shared the political experience of the older generation), and indeed they are disengaged from all institutional associations. At the same time that they are withdrawn from causes (social manifestations), they are deeply committed to the individual experience and one's identity with the environment (by contrast with the Dada group, whose sense of estrangement led them away from participation)" (p. 73). See also Raoul Hausmann, "Aussichten oder Ende des Neodadaismus," in *Das war Dada—Dichtungen und Dokumente*, ed. P. Schifferli (Zurich: Verlag der Arche, 1963). The old Dadaist Hausmann is much more explicit in his assessment of "pop art": "Among many other things, Dada was an attitude of protest against bourgeois and intellectual traditions. Neodadaism is definitely not that . . ." (p. 161). "Neodadaism? No, simply depressionism" (p. 164).

13. Dwight McDonald, "A Theory of Mass Culture," in *Mass Culture: Popular Arts in America*, eds. B. Rosenberg and D. M. White (New York: Free Press, 1967): "Mass culture is imposed from above. It is fabricated by technicians hired by businessmen; its audiences are passive consumers, their participation limited to the choice between buying and not buying" (p. 60). See Alberto Arbasino, *Off-Off* (Milan: Feltrinelli, 1968). Following the tracks of McDonald, Arbasino completes the idea: ". . . By now, popular means that this culture is produced industrially for the masses (by smooth intellectuals who work for RCA and CBS) . . . and is no longer the spontaneous expression of the masses, as was once the case with *la bela gigogin*, the carpets of the Valtellina, or the stone saints at the crossroads . . ." (p. 23).

14. See Warren Weaver, *Science and Complexity*; and also Lewis Feuer, "The Principle of Simplicity," in *Philosophy of Science*, 24:2 (April, 1957); and Georg Schlesinger, "The Principle of Simplicity and Verifiability," in *Philosophy of Science*, 26:1 (January, 1959).

CHAPTER SIXTEEN

1. The study of the mishaps encountered by "ideal models" when they are transferred to reality has not yet developed satisfactorily. In the field of the sociology of public housing, the most acute criticism (or rather self-criticism) is that by Robert K. Merton in his famous essay "The Social Psychology of Housing," in *Current Trends in Social Psychology*, ed. W. Dennis (Pittsburgh: University of Pittsburgh Press, 1948). The later work of American sociologists was directed almost exclusively toward the study of problems on a microsociological level (perhaps because of the difficulties encountered and announced by Merton); and to tell the truth they have produced brilliant results. Examples of this tendency are the works done in the footsteps of the precursors Svend Riemer and F. Stupart Chapin by N. L. Mintz, A. E. Scheflen, Robert Sommer, Bernard Steinzor, and Edward T. Hall. Recently, German sociology (or rather psychosociology) has shown a vigorous reawakening of interest in urban reality. See Heide Berndt, Alfred Lorenzer, and Klaus Horn, *Architektur als Ideologie* (Frankfurt: Suhrkamp Verlag, 1968). The authors, who are collaborators of Alexander Mitscherlich's at the Sigmund Freud Institut in Frankfurt, are once again trying to initiate criticism of the urban situation in bourgeois society on the macrosociological level. In our opinion, results have been rather modest. Their mistake is that they have made the criticism of "functionalism" in architecture and in urbanistics the nucleus of their criticism of the urban situation today. It is an approach that arrives too late. Especially when we recall that the debate on "functionalism" was taken to its extreme consequences ten years ago by the architects and urban planners in CIAM (Congressi Internazionali

di Architettura Moderna). On this matter, see Giancarlo De Carlo, *Questioni di architettura e urbanistica* (Urbino: Argalia, 1965), particularly the chapter "L'ultimo convegno dei CIAM con una memoria sui contenuti dell'architettura moderna," pp. 60*ff*. In the debate on "functionalism," an important role was played by the difficulty in establishing clearly the real content of that notion. The truth of that is also shown by an investigation of its historical origin. See E. R. De Zurko, *Origins of Functionalist Theory* (New York: Columbia University Press, 1957). It is evident that historians, critics, and theoreticians of architecture and urbanistics today are continuing to use the notion of "functionalism" only for convenience of language, and not because they believe in its semantic correspondence to the phenomenon they wish to describe. In the books by the German psychologists, on the other hand, "functionalism" is treated as a definitely established notion; but in reality they are arguing wth a scarecrow. A Marxist criticism of the interpretation of Mitscherlich's collaborators may be found in P. Neitzke, "Die Agenten der Kulturkritik isolieren!" in *Kapitalistischer Städtebau*, eds. H. G. Helms and J. Janssen (Neuwied and Berlin: Luchterhand, 1970).

2. "Praxiology," as Kotarbiński defines it, "is the general theory of efficient action." See Tadeusz Kotarbiński, *Praxiology: An Introduction to the Science of Efficient Action* (Oxford: Pergamon Press, 1965). This author has tried to establish a meeting point between two currents of thought—logical empiricism and Marxism, or even Dewey's pragmatism and Marxism—which, after Lenin's criticism in *Materialism and Empirio-Criticism* were usually considered irreconcilable. Another important work, a precursor of this direction, is the one by Giulio Preti, *Praxis ed empirismo* (Turin: Einaudi, 1957). In any case, the "general theory of design praxis" has still to be developed. Despite its undeniable interest, the praxiology of Kotarbiński cannot serve as the point of departure for the elaboration of such a theory. Because of its speculative abstractness, it is not very operable. It magisterially defines the specific methodological needs for the design of efficient action; but it leaves us without any help if we want to know whether such action is legitimate within the context

of a given society. This is a point not to be underestimated. The new theory, at least as we imagine it, must have as its fulcrum the problem of the ethical and practical—let us say *tout-court* political—implications of design and planning. Of all the efforts made to clarify the relationship between action and critical consciousness, it is in Gramsci's philosophy of praxis that we find the most valid and fruitful beginnings. See Antonio Gramsci, *Il materialismo storico e la filosofia di Benedetto Croce*, 8th ed. (Turin: Einaudi, 1966). For the antecedents of Gramsci's philosophy of praxis, see M. Tronti, "Tra materialismo dialettico e filosofia della prassi," in *La città futura*, eds. A. Caracciolo and G. Scalia (Milan: Feltrinelli, 1959). As we know, this aspect of Gramsci's thought does not enjoy general approval today. The Czech K. Kossik, for example, maintains that Gramsci left his philosophy of praxis in a sketchy state, whereas we consider it the essential nucleus of his doctrine. In our opinion, the main impulses for new Marxist hermeneutics (not only retrospective but also prospective) have their point of departure here. This is particularly evident when we connect the philosophy of praxis with another of Gramsci's important mental constructs: the categories he introduced to describe the bipolar reality of every social infrastructure. On the one hand, "political society," i.e., the dominion exercised by means of a coercive state apparatus; and on the other hand the "civil society" in the Hegelian sense, i.e., dominion by means of private, noncoercive organisms. See Antonio Gramsci, *Gli intellettuali e l'organizzazione della cultura*. See also the Letter to Tatiana, dated September 7, 1931, in Gramsci, *Lettere dall'carcere*, 2d ed. (Turin: Einaudi, 1968), p. 481. Usually, the more advanced nations have a vigorous "political society" but also a very influential and consistent "civil society." In these cases, *before* trying to suppress political society, elementary tactical caution counsels action directed toward weakening the hegemony of the civil society. At the same time, by means of long, stubborn, and all-pervading work of persuasion, one should try to render the hegemony of a new civil society ever more intelligible, acceptable, and even desirable. This caution does not seem justified in the underdeveloped countries, where civil society normally does not exist. It is therefore possible (as was the case in the Russian revolution and might be the case today in the less developed countries of Latin America, Asia, and Africa) to overthrow the existing political society and *thereafter* develop the new civil society through the mediation of a period of "statolatry." See Gramsci, *Passato e presente*, 6th ed. (Turin: Einaudi, 1966), p. 166; and Gramsci, *Il risorgimento*, 9th ed. (Turin: Einaudi, 1966), p. 70. Clearly Gramsci's idea of "statolatry" is subject to a potential risk: Many might identify it with Stalinism. It might therefore be believed that this repressive (in our opinion pathological) modality of socialism is a necessary step for all countries lacking a civil society. See R. Mondolfo, *Umanismo di Marx* (Turin: Einaudi, 1968), pp. 398*ff*. Nevertheless, it must be recognized that Gramsci himself, in his famous passage on this subject, spoke against that possibility of deviant interpretation: "Statolatry . . . is nothing but the normal form of 'state-life' . . . it must not be left to itself and, above all, it must not become theoretical fanaticism and be conceived of as 'perpetual': it must be criticized precisely so that it may develop and produce new forms of state-life" (p. 166). The various nuances that we can discern in Gramsci's idea of statolatry absolutely do not change the fact that his bipolar conception of the infrastructure of society constitutes a basic and new development in the traditional debate, which is very current today, on the strategy of revolution. Gramsci's approach overcomes dialectically, not eclectically, many of the most bitter differences of opinions on the subject. According to this view, completely diverse and even opposed strategies can be equally right. Everything depends on the kind of relationship that exists between civil society and political society in the system that is to be overthrown. It is precisely in this interpretative context that the theory of design praxis suddenly becomes not only feasible but urgently necessary. The questions it is supposed to answer are many and extremely complex. If it is true that there are diverse superstructural modalities and therefore diverse revolutionary strategies, that obviously must have a decisive influence on the definition of the role—or rather, as we shall see, of the roles—of the designer. Guided by Gramsci, one can say that the designer, inasmuch as he is "an organic intellectual," that is to say, inasmuch as he is a "commissioner" of the dominant group (Gramsci, *Gli intellettuali e l'organizzazione della cultura*, p. 9), fulfills his task principally in the bosom of civil society and as a function thereof. But it is a mistake to believe, as is usually the case, that the designer is always and necessarily a "commissioner" of the dominant group already in power. He can also be a "salesman" for the group that is trying to become dominant, and which is trying to destroy the old power to substitute it with a new. It is possible for him to assume the intermediary role between the "agents" and the "managers" of the revolution (Gramsci, *L'ordine nuovo 1919–20*, 3d ed., Turin: Einaudi, 1970). Nevertheless, that role is not always realized in the same way. Here too, we can say that there are as many forms of design praxis as there are of revolutionary strategy.

3. See E. M. Rogers, *Esperienza di un corso universitario: L'utopia della realtà* (Bari: Leonardo da Vinci, 1965). In this introductory essay to a course given at the Facoltà di architettura del politecnico di Milano, the architect Rogers writes: "We know such pedagogical choices bring with them the danger that young people will take hold of them superficially and will end up by bringing the vital impulse beyond utopia to confuse it with an irrational dream, with a chimera, and in this specific case will become architects of 'castles in the air' instead of being the builders of a new environment for a renewed mankind. Therefore, my course is based on the conceptual slogan of a 'utopia of reality,' where the inseparable association of the two nouns seeks to establish the dialectical synthesis of the two terms which, considered separately, would be irremediably opposed" (p. 14). The proposal is correct but incomplete. There is lacking, for example, that which is present in the "concrete utopia" of Bloch: the conviction that the "dialectical synthesis" between utopia and reality is attainable only through innovative action on the web of the existing social order. See Pierluigi Giordani, *Il futuro dell'utopia* (Bologna: Calderini, 1969). The author develops a "utopia of the possible" which he defines, in an urbanistic vein, as "a programming that is not very different in capitalist and in socialist cities" (p. 3). On the subject of "design-utopia" and reality, see

also Filiberto Menna, *Profezia di una società estetica* (Rome: Lerici, 1968), p. 131*ff.*

4. Ernst Bloch, *Das Prinzip Hoffnung*, I, p. 16.

5. *Ibid.*, p. 256.

6. *Ibid.*, II, p. 724.

7. In the lectures he held during the winter semester of 1960–61 at the university of Tübingen, Bloch saw fit to attenuate his intransigence toward empiricism. On that occasion he said, "Never lose touch with the *process* of empiricism"—*Tübingen Einleitung in die Philosophie*, I (Frankfurt: Suhrkamp, 1953), p. 157. It is a step forward, no doubt, but at the same time it is once again limited, once again sealed off by the emphasis on the word "process."

8. Bloch, *op. cit.*, p. 157.

9. On the subject of "logical silence" and dissent, see the very stimulating book by Franco Spisani, *Logica della contestazione* (Bologna: Cappelli, 1969).

10. H. M. Enzensberger, Rudi Dutschke, Bert Rabehl, and Christian Semler, "Ein Gespräch über die Zukunft," in *Kursbuch*, 14 (August, 1968), pp. 146–74.

11. That consideration is valid only for the messianic utopians of the extraparliamentary opposition; the same cannot be said for that other group of messianic utopians known to the public as hippies. Not even the utopianism of these out-and-out rebels can resist the test of concreteness. In any case, it is not advisable to believe blindly in the good faith and even less in the political progressivism of all representatives of the hippie world. At the round-table discussion organized by the review *Oracle* in San Francisco in 1967 (a transcript of which was printed in *Notes from the New Underground*, ed. J. Kornbluth (New York: Viking Press, 1968), Timothy Leary, C. Snyder, and Alan Watts, incited by the sarcastic and lucid remarks of the poet Allen Ginsberg, discussed the future of their movement. At the beginning of the discussion, Ginsberg made an incidental reference to the opinion of the Berkeley student leader Mario Savio, according to whom "the things that move large crowds were righteousness, moral outrage, and anger, righteous anger" (p. 122). This opinion, as banal as it is

correct, is enough to unleash an angry reaction from the "high priest" Leary. "Well: let's stop here. The implication of that statement is: we want a mass movement. Mass movements make no sense to me, and I want no part of mass movements. I think this is the error that the leftist activists are making. I see them as young men with menopausal minds. They are repeating the same dreary quarrels and conflicts for power of the thirties and the forties, of the trade union movement, of Trotskyism and so forth. I think they should be sanctified, drop out, find their own center, turn on, and above all avoid mass movements, mass leadership, mass followers. I see that there is a great difference—I say completely incompatible difference—between the leftist activist movement and the psychedelic religious movement" (p. 123). And when one of the participants asked whether the world of the future will continue to be based on technology like the present world, Leary answered affirmatively, quickly adding that technology—that is to say, all the technical-productive infrastructures—have to be swept away from the face of the earth and transferred to a more suitable place: underground. Because, he says apodictically, everything that is metallic belongs underground. Leary does not stop there. He also foresees that in this buried technological universe, work will be done by a new species of primate, which, though derived from the human species, cannot really be called human. The "real" human beings, those who have successfully liberated themselves from "plastic society" through the use of drugs, can continue to enjoy their bucolic lives on the surface of the earth, making use of the products of the not so bucolic work that those others are doing underground. We can quickly see what lies behind this utopianism: an awesome authoritarian ideology. The world foreseen by Leary is in fact permeated with social Darwinism. His hostile attitude toward the masses assumes a very precise meaning here. His is a dream of dominance, of dominance of the masses. In his petit bourgeois megalomania, he conceives of a world in keeping with his rancor. Recently Leary, who escaped from a penal institution in California and went to Algeria, seems to be moving in a political direction that is closer to the extraparliamentary left. His change of orientation does not of course invalidate our comments on his earlier positions.

12. See the recent essay by Romano Luperini, "Gli intellettuali di sinistra e l'ideologia della ricostruzione nel dopoguerra," in *Ideologie*, 8 (1969), 55–104.

13. Elio Vittorini, "Politica e cultura," in *Politecnico*, 31–32, (July-August, 1946).

POSTSCRIPT

1. In his essays on the *imagination materielle*, G. Bachelard demonstrated admirably that in the formative processes of verbal symbolization, especially in those dealing with air, water, and earth, nature often appears to be the target of our most aggressive impulses. See Gaston Bachelard, *L'eau et les rêves: Essai sur imagination de la matière* (Paris: J. Corti, 1942); *L'air et les songes: Essai sur l'imagination du mouvement* (Paris: J. Corti, 1943); *La Terre et les rêveries de la volonté* (Paris: J. Corti, 1948); *La terre et les rêveries du repos* (Paris: J. Corti, 1948).

2. See "Parade de l'environment," in *Urbaniser la lutte de classe* (Paris: Utopie, 1970). The text, presented in June 1970 at the International Design Conference, Aspen, Colorado, is a polemical denunciation of the bourgeois ideology implicit in the "fashion of ecology." The authors define the current crusade for the salvation of the environment as "a social drug, a new opium of the people" (p. 52).

3. The fashion of ecology is now diffused internationally, but the epicenter, the hearth, is located in the United States. It was officially launched by the public action taken by President Nixon at the beginning of 1970. See "National Environment Policy Act of 1969 (Statement, Remarks, and Announcement. January 1, 1970)," in *Weekly Compilation of Presidential Documents*, 6–1 (January 5, 1970); "President's State of the Union Message (January 22, 1970)," in *Vital Speeches of the Day*, 36:8 (February 1970); "Control of Air and Water Pollution at Federal Facilities (Statement and Executive Order. February 4, 1970)" in *Weekly Compilation of Presidential Documents*," 6–6 (February 9, 1970); "Environmental Quality (Remarks, February 10, 1970)," in *Weekly Compilation of Presidential Documents*, 6, 7 (February 16, 1970). The launching was aided by a press campaign that very deftly and

quickly made itself the interpreter of the presidential action. In fact, from one day to the next, as though they were responding to a *Diktat,* the most important organs of the American press—*Time, Newsweek, Life, Fortune, Business Week,* and even *Playboy*—all became very concerned with the subject.

4. Robert Heilbroner, "Ecological Armageddon," *The New York Review of Books,* 14:8 (April 23, 1970), p. 3.

INDEX

135

Tomás Maldonado (1922–2018) was one of the most significant design thinkers of the twentieth century. A leading figure in the Argentinean avant-garde movement of Arte Concreto and editor of the journal *Nueva Visión,* he was best known for his work at the German Hochschule für Gestaltung Ulm, also known as the Ulm School, where he adapted the spirit of the Bauhaus to the aesthetic, sociological, political, and economic demands of the late twentieth century, becoming one of the first designers to engage with cybernetics, semiotics, and emerging digital technologies. He moved to Milan in 1970 and became a leading public intellectual as well as professor of environmental design at Polytechnic University of Milan. He wrote a series of books that critically assess culture and technology.

Mario Domandi was professor of Italian at Vassar College.

Larry Busbea is associate professor of art history at the University of Arizona, Tucson, and author of *Topologies: The Urban Utopia in France, 1960–1970* and *The Responsive Environment: Design, Aesthetics, and the Human in the 1970s* (Minnesota, 2020).